365 BABY CARE TIPS

Everything You Need to Know
about Caring for Your Baby
in the First Year of Life

by Penny Warner

Author of *Smart Start for Your Baby,*
Baby Play and Learn, and *Baby Birthday Parties*

 **Meadowbrook Press**

Distributed by Simon & Schuster
New York

Library of Congress Cataloging-in-Publication Data

Warner, Penny.
  365 baby care tips : everything you need to know about caring for your
baby in the first year of life / by Penny Warner.
     p. cm.
  Includes bibliographical references and index.
  ISBN 0-88166-430-8 (Meadowbrook)
    1. Infants—Care. 2. Infants—Health and hygiene. 3. Parent and infant. 4.
Parenting. I. Title: Three hundred and sixty five baby care tips. II. Title.

RJ61.W294 2002
649.1'22—dc21   2002075163

Editorial Director: Christine Zuchora-Walske
Editor: Joseph Gredler
Proofreader: Angela Wiechmann
Production Manager: Paul Woods
Text Design: Peggy Bates
Cover Photos: Comstock Images, Getty Images, and RubberBall Productions
Illustrations: Susan Spellman
Index: Beverlee Day

Published by Meadowbrook Press, 5451 Smetana Drive, Minnetonka, Minnesota
55343

BOOK TRADE DISTRIBUTION by Simon & Schuster, a division of Simon and
Schuster, Inc., 1230 Avenue of the Americas, New York, NY, 10020

The contents of this book have been reviewed and checked for accuracy and appropriateness. However, the authors, editors, reviewers, and publisher disclaim all
responsibility arising from any adverse effects that occur or might occur as a result
of the inappropriate application of any information contained in this book. If you
have a question about the appropriateness of the information provided in this
book, consult your health care professional.

05 04 03 02   13 12 11 10 9 8 7 6 5 4 3 2 1

Printed in the United States of America

Dedication

To my babies, Matthew and Rebecca,
and their wonderful dad, Tom

Acknowledgments

Thanks so much to all who contributed their expertise, especially Shannon Barry, Colleen Casey, Melanie Ellington, Tiffany Gaddis, Anne Gilbertson, Claire Johnson, Cindy Jones, Holly Kralj, Rena Leith, Vanessa Matiski, Dana Mentick, Taya Morrison, Cindy Murphy, Ann Parker, Connie Pike, Chris Saunders, Barbara Shabaniani, Vicki Stadelhofer, Barbara Swec, Judy Takeda, Cara Varon, Mary Warner, Susan Warner, Simonie Webster, and Susan Westerlund.

Contents

Foreword

365 Baby Care Tips offers new parents an accessible guide to enjoying and caring for their baby during the first year (and beyond). The handy format enables quick reference to important material when time is at a premium. The friendly tone makes for easy reading while parents are feeding or holding their baby. The quick tips, bonus tips, and caution tips make readers feel like they're sitting around a coffee table sharing advice with family and friends.

Tidbits of wisdom are especially entertaining, such as leaving a vacuum cleaner out to suggest to guests that cleaning is about to happen (even if it isn't). Choosing a special song for a new baby is a delightful way to emphasize the child's uniqueness. Readers will also find helpful tips on enhancing communication with their babies by using sign language.

Though targeted primarily to parents of babies from birth to one year, *365 Baby Care Tips* contains much information that is relevant beyond the first year. This book would also benefit the expectant parent and would make an excellent shower or baby gift.

It is generally agreed that the first year of life brings more changes than any other. How handy to have a comprehensive, friendly guide to help new parents during this incredible time. Enjoy!

Paula M. Kelly, M.D.

Introduction

Welcoming a new baby into the family is one of the most exciting journeys of your life. Like most journeys, it's nice to have a map—and there's nothing wrong with asking for directions along the way. A guidebook helps you avoid getting lost, warns you about bumpy spots along the road, and alerts you to milestones that shouldn't be missed. That's what *365 Baby Care Tips* is all about. It helps you maneuver the curves, detours, and occasional roadblocks of parenthood by providing you with hundreds of practical tips and expert opinions on everything you need to know in the first year of your baby's life.

365 Baby Care Tips is arranged by topics, beginning with information you'll need when you first bring your baby home. The early chapters focus on bonding with your baby, adjusting to your new life, staying connected with your partner, introducing your baby to the rest of the family, and understanding the basics of baby care. Subsequent chapters provide helpful tips on diapering, bathing, sleeping, crying, breastfeeding, formula-feeding, solid foods, teething, baby equipment, discipline, and returning to work. You'll learn how to keep your baby safe and healthy, and you'll discover fun ways to enhance your baby's development.

In addition to the numerous "subtips" within each numbered section, you'll find several "quick tips" provided by experienced parents who've shared their best secrets. Chapters are arranged in an easy-to-read format that makes information convenient and accessible.

Sometimes the fantasy of enjoying a new baby doesn't quite match the reality of nighttime feedings, blowout diapers, and sleep deprivation. If you're wondering how you'll ever adjust to the challenges of parenthood, you're doing the right thing. You're consulting a comprehensive resource that will help you navigate a steady course.

The goal of *365 Baby Care Tips* is to help you and your baby make the biggest adjustments of your lives. We appreciate the opportunity to help you guide your baby on the journey through early childhood, and we wish you safe passage on the road to becoming a confident and caring parent.

Chapter 1:
Adjusting to Parenthood

1. Baby and Parent: Bonding for Life

A close attachment between you and your baby begins at birth (and to some extent in utero) and continues to grow over time. To ensure an early attachment with your baby, you should do the following.

Hold your baby. The best way to begin the bonding process is to hold your baby as much and as long as you like—no matter what your relatives and friends might say about spoiling him. You can't spoil your baby in the first year of life.

Look at your baby. Make eye contact with your newborn and watch his eyes meet yours. He may be attracted to your hairline at first (because of the contrast), but soon he'll be gazing lovingly into your eyes. Bat your eyes and move them around to help him focus attention there.

Nurse your baby. Breastfeed your baby, if possible, or hold him every time you formula-feed him. This will enhance the feelings of attachment between you. Never prop a bottle to feed your baby. This will not only impair his attachment and overall development, he may choke on the milk as it pours down his throat.

Touch your baby. Your baby responds to your touch. In fact, he thrives on it. Massage him, stroke him, caress him, and handle him throughout the day. Your touch helps him grow in every way.

Wear your baby. Carry your baby around in a front pack or sling. Your arms will be free to do things while your baby is rocked and comforted next to your body. It's an easy and convenient way to keep your baby close to your heart.

Spend time with your baby. Enjoy your baby by chatting, singing, rocking, and sharing special moments with him each day. The time really does pass quickly, so enjoy it while it lasts.

2. Quick Tip: Baby Secrets

The way I got acquainted with my baby was by telling her my thoughts, plans, and secrets throughout the day. She was such a good listener. I really felt like she understood me, even though I know she didn't. As I talked to her and shared myself with her, she started to become my best friend. She still is to this day.

—Mia T.

3. Baby Yourself: Taking Care of Your Physical Needs

Before you can effectively take care of your baby, you need to take care of yourself.

Eat well. A good diet will help you feel better, give you the energy you need, and provide good nutrition for your baby if you're breastfeeding. Avoid alcohol, too much caffeine, any drug not recommended by your doctor, and any food that seems to give you—or your baby—indigestion.

Dress comfortably. Don't try to wear your pre-pregnancy clothes for a few weeks after the birth. They usually don't fit well, and that can be depressing. Instead, wear loose, comfortable clothes such as breastfeeding tops and elastic-waist pants.

4. Quick Tip: Nap When Your Baby Naps

Every time your baby goes down for a nap, take one yourself. Forget the housecleaning, the laundry, the cooking—everything. Sleep deprivation is a form of torture, so don't do it to yourself! Nap when your baby naps. It was the best advice I got.

—Ann P.

5. Quick Tip: Cesarean Lap

If you've had a cesarean section and can't hold your baby on your lap without pain, put a firm pillow on your lap first, then hold your baby. If you want to breastfeed, stack several pillows on your lap so your baby can reach your breast easily and so you can remain comfortable. This also works well for mothers with bad backs. If your baby falls asleep on the pillow, you can easily transfer her to her crib without disturbing her.

—*Barbara S.*

6. Baby Yourself: Taking Care of Your Emotional Needs

Talk about your feelings. Express your emotions instead of keeping them bottled up. Don't be afraid to let others know what's causing you concern. You'll be better able to deal with your emotions if you get them out in the open.

Take breaks. You may feel so attached to your baby, you'll wonder if the two of you are still connected by an invisible umbilical cord. Take a break from your baby now and then to remember how it feels to be by yourself.

Just say no! If you don't feel like doing something, politely say no. If you don't feel up to having friends or family over, don't. If your mother is being too pushy, gently ask her to back off. It will help you feel more in control of your life.

7. Quick Tip: Cry-Mommy

The first few days after I got home from the hospital, I found myself weeping every time I felt overwhelmed—and sometimes for no reason at all. One day my mother-in-law criticized the way I was diapering my baby. I just burst into tears. But suddenly she backed off! Not only did it feel good to cry, it reminded everyone around me that I needed some space.

—Karen D.

8. Quick Tip: Mellow Mom

My baby seemed to be stressed when I was, so I began listening to relaxation tapes. The ocean sounds were really soothing. I also did deep breathing exercises. The calmer I felt, the calmer my baby felt.

—Cindy M.

9. Mother Yourself: Simplifying Your Life

To deal effectively with the dramatic changes during the first weeks at home with your baby, simplify your life and get help with household jobs.

Take a maternity leave. Take time off from work to make sure you get off to a great start with your baby. Extend your leave as long as possible. If you can't take a leave of absence, consider reducing your work schedule. (See Chapter 23.)

Get help. In addition to your partner, ask your parents, parents-in-law, relatives, close friends, or a doula to help out during the first few weeks. Have your helpers do chores while you and your partner take care of the baby.

Don't worry about the mess. The laundry, the dishes, the mess—they'll still be there when you finally have time and energy to deal with them. Your baby is changing every minute, so enjoy that time first.

10. Baby Times Two: Twins and Multiples

Double the pleasure, double the work? Having twins or multiples is exciting, but it can also be overwhelming. Here are some tips on coping with two or more babies at the same time.

- Get two (or more) of everything, if you can afford it, and think about what can be shared, such as the changing table.

- Try to feed your babies at the same time, so you'll have time to do other things.

- Get help from anyone who will volunteer time and equipment.
- Join a multiples group such as the Mothers of Twins Club.
- Treat your babies as individuals. Emphasize the things that make them unique, and encourage others to do the same. Try not to compare your babies.

11. Quick Tip: Similar but Different

Even before my twins were born, I joined the Mothers of Twins Club in my city. They gave me a head start on what to expect. The best thing I learned was to treat my babies individually, not as a pair, and to help them develop their own identities. Although I was tempted, I didn't dress them the same way, didn't name them rhyming names, and didn't talk to them as if they were one person. I called each child by name (instead of saying, "the twins"), and I made an effort to spend alone time with each of them. I'm sure they'll be close—they really love being with each other—but I also hope they'll appreciate how unique they are as human beings.

—Chris S.

12. The Chosen One: Your Adopted Baby

Adopting a baby creates special rewards and concerns that are unique to each situation.

Be involved. If possible, try to be involved in the pregnancy to ensure good prenatal care. If you're adopting privately, help the mother choose a childbirth class, and participate in the birth.

Make arrangements. Carefully plan when and where you'll receive the baby.

Begin bonding. When you get your baby, spend as much time as you can with him to establish bonding.

Get support. Join an adoption support group to share questions and answers with other adoptive parents. (See Appendix I.)

13. Quick Tip: The Chosen One

My husband didn't want to tell our child he was adopted until he got older, but I'd read some books that recommended letting your child know right from the start. That way he'd grow up used to the idea. We told our son he was special because we got to choose him. We also decided to help him find his birth parents when he got older, if he wanted to.

—Joanne D.

14. Role Overload: Single Parenting

Single parenting is like having twice the workload with half the help. Here are some tips to help you cope as a single parent.

Compromise. Try not to do it all yourself. Make compromises and accept the fact that you can't be everything to everyone.

Get help. Ask relatives, friends, and other parents to help you out, and accept all offers of assistance.

Take a break. You'll need some time alone to gather your energy and refresh yourself.

15. Quick Tip: Singles Unite

My marriage broke up while I was pregnant, so I was a single mom from the beginning. I thought I could handle it, but I really felt overloaded. I joined a single mothers' group and got all sorts of tips and support from the group members. They even had a babysitting co-op that helped each of us get some time to ourselves. Some of those women are still my friends today, years later. I don't think I could have done it without them.

—Natalie L.

16. Children with Disabilities: Where to Find Help

If you have a child with a disability, here are some tips for finding out more information and getting assistance.

Get connected. Contact an appropriate organization for referrals, information, and support. (See Appendix I.)

Join up. Join a support group to share your concerns and to learn that you're not alone. (See Appendix I.)

Research. Read and inform yourself about your baby's disability, and begin intervention and education as soon as possible. Talk to your doctor and other health care professionals.

Relax. Realize that your child will grow, develop, and learn, but perhaps in a different way.

Easy does it. Take it one day at a time, and enjoy everything your special baby has to offer.

Let it out. Allow yourself to cry. Your emotions are valid, and you have the right to express them.

Take your time. Give yourself time to deal with your emotions and your situation. Having a disabled child causes parents to go through a number of emotions similar to dealing with a death in the family.

Don't neglect yourself. Take care of your needs so you can take care of your baby.

Avoid the guilt. Don't feel guilty about your child's disability or for not being the perfect parent.

Write it down. Keep a journal to express your thoughts and feelings.

Make notes. Keep a record of your baby's growth and development so you can see the ways she's changing.

17. Quick Tip: Educate People

My baby was born deaf. I used sign language with her early on, and I got a lot of stares from people. At first their rudeness really bothered me, but eventually I realized that maybe they were just curious. So I began telling them about my daughter and how we communicate. Educating people was much more satisfying than getting mad at them for their ignorance.

—Connor W.

18. Getting Your Figure Back through Exercise

Exercising after childbirth is another great way to get back into your pre-pregnancy clothes. Even if you didn't exercise during pregnancy, it's never too late to begin.

Start slowly. If you were active before delivery, you can resume regular exercise when you feel ready. Begin with light exercise, such as light aerobics or brisk walking, or continue with your yoga practice. If you weren't active before delivery, start by walking a little each day and increase your activity over time. Talk to your care provider about how to proceed.

Housework workout. Put a little more energy into those household chores, and soon you'll not only have a clean home, you'll have a trimmer body, stronger muscles, and fewer pounds.

Stay positive. Exercise can help you feel better psychologically, too. If you have mild postpartum depression, try listening to your favorite music or watching your favorite TV show while you workout.

Kegels. By strengthening your pelvic floor muscles, these exercises improve urinary control, promote healing after an episiotomy, and may improve the quality of sexual intercourse. Constrict the muscles of your vagina and perineum, hold for several seconds, and release. (Repeat several times a day.) You can begin Kegels immediately after delivery.

19. Quick Tip: Baby Gym

I took my baby to a baby gym class where we both got all the exercise we needed. It got me out of the house, and I met other mothers who were looking for ways to get back in shape. My baby loved being around other babies, and I lost weight doing my exercises and chasing him around the class.

—Jennifer R.

20. Quick Tip: Baby Workout

I didn't feel up to exercising after I had my C-section. I had a lot of pain from the incision, and my abdomen was generally sore. What finally got me going was my baby. When he cried, nothing calmed him except walking and rocking. Doing this several times a day got me back into shape pretty fast. It was good for my waist, abdomen, legs, heart—and baby, too.

—Melissa A.

21. Quick Tip: Chocolate Medicine

One of the nurses told me chocolate was bad for nursing mothers, and she took away my box of candy! I found out later that no particular food is bad for breastfeeding mothers, although some foods may upset a mother's stomach or cause minor problems with baby's digestion. I'm convinced chocolate is good for nursing mothers. It gives us energy and pleasure, and it contains antioxidants that help prevent certain diseases. I say, bring on the chocolate medicine!

—Courtney B.

22. Getting Your Figure Back through Breastfeeding and Nutrition

One of your biggest personal concerns after childbirth may be getting your figure back. The good news is you'll probably lose fifty to seventy-five percent of your pregnancy weight immediately after delivery. For those extra pounds, consider the following.

Breastfeed. Breastfeeding burns about a thousand calories a day, and it causes the release of hormones that help your uterus contract to its normal size and shape. Breastfeeding is also great for your baby.

Eat well. Most breastfeeding women need about two thousand calories per day. Eating a well-balanced diet is essential for you and your baby. Talk to your care provider about a healthy nutrition plan.

Avoid strict dieting. If you're breastfeeding, a strict diet could be unhealthy for you and your baby. Instead, eat healthy foods, drink lots of fluids, and begin your diet *after* you've finished breastfeeding. By then you may not need to lose much weight.

Don't expect miracles. Getting your figure back takes time, so be patient. After all, it took nine months to put on all that weight! The last five to ten pounds can be stubborn, so cut yourself a little slack.

23. Getting Your Figure Back by Inviting a Friend

If you're not very self-motivated, you may want to recruit a buddy to help you stay on schedule with your exercise routine.

Include your baby. You can set your baby on your legs while doing leg lifts, put him on your stomach while doing sit-ups, lay him on the floor while doing toe-touches, and so on. Get a jogging stroller so you can take him for a walk or run around the neighborhood. Getting outside will be good for both of you.

Take a class. Signing up for a formal exercise class will get you out of the house, give you some time away from your baby, and help you regain your figure with a regular, disciplined routine. You'll enjoy spending time around other people maintaining their physical fitness.

Find a friend. Exercising with a friend will keep you motivated as you spend time talking about babies, problems, and mutual interests.

24. Three's a Crowd?

Adjusting to life with a baby is challenging—and stressful—for any couple.

Communicate your concerns. Talk to each other about how things are going, what you want, and what you might be missing.

Share your feelings. Don't be afraid to express your emotions. You may find you have many feelings in common (both positive and negative).

Listen to each other. Part of communicating is listening—really listening—to each other. Make eye contact, give feedback, and ask questions to clarify things.

Use body language. Don't just talk. Use body language such as cuddling, handholding, massage, kissing, even sex—if the other person is interested.

25. Quick Tip: Make a Date

After our baby was born, we promised ourselves a weekly date to remember what it was like to be a couple. We spent most of the time talking about the baby, but it was still nice to have that romantic evening together. And I couldn't wait to get back to my baby at the end of the evening!
—Simonie W.

26. Make My Day: Special Surprises

Here are a few more tips for keeping your romance alive and well.

- Put on your favorite music.
- Make a romantic dinner for two.
- Surprise your partner with a special gift.
- Get a babysitter and go out.
- Give a massage or manicure.
- Wear something sexy.
- Mail a romantic card.
- Compliment each other.
- Bring home flowers or balloons.

27. Quick Tip: Blind Date

To spice up our marriage after our baby was born, I set up a "blind" date. I sent my husband a note to meet "Brittany" at a romantic restaurant after work. He knew it was from me (it came from my e-mail address), but he got totally into the fantasy. I arranged for a babysitter, put on some sexy clothes, and was waiting at the table when he arrived. He even brought flowers and candy! Needless to say, the date continued at home—behind closed doors—at least until the baby started crying.

—Kelly V.

28. Back in the Saddle? Or Saddle Sore?

Don't rush the sex. Getting back into the swing of things takes time. You may feel tired and sore and not ready for sex, and you may feel guilty for not being ready. Your partner may worry about hurting you during sex. Try other ways of sharing intimacy during the transition period after delivery.

Caution: If you're having serious relationship problems after the baby is born, consider seeing a family therapist to help you work through your issues.

29. Quick Tip: Off the Pedestal

My husband had trouble getting back into sex after the baby came. When I asked him what was wrong, he said he was having trouble with the "mother" image of me. I was no longer his sexy wife; I was a responsible and maternal woman. We had a long talk about this. I tried to convince him that nothing had changed, but he was still hesitant in his lovemaking. Finally, I got a babysitter, rented a hotel room, kidnapped my husband, and spent the night reminding him of the sexy woman I was and hopefully always will be.

—Risa L.

Chapter 2:
Meeting the Family

30. "Da Da!": Becoming a Dad

Fathers can bond with their newborns just as effectively as mothers—if they're given the same opportunities.

Contribute. Have Dad help set up the baby's room before the birth. He can build shelves, paint walls, hang a mobile, and so on. Dads tend to prefer hands-on tasks when preparing for baby.

Comfort. Encourage Dad to pick up your crying baby and comfort her. The more Dad responds to your baby, the more attached he'll feel.

Chat. Remind Dad to talk to your baby about anything—even sports! Men are usually not as verbal with their children, and they may have to be reminded to chat with their babies once in a while.

Cuddle. Encourage Dad to wear your baby in a front pack or sling, so the two of them can have some cuddling time. This way Dad can do his chores and keep your baby company at the same time.

Commend. Instead of criticizing Dad's methods of baby care, praise him for his efforts. If one of his parenting techniques bothers you, gently suggest another way.

31. Daddy Time Means Play Time

Experts today believe that, aside from the ability to breastfeed, fathers and mothers are equal in their ability to parent. But there are some differences in style. Fathers tend to be louder, friskier, and more roughhousing than mothers. Here are some things to keep in mind while playing with your baby.

- Don't be too rough. Although babies are basically strong and resilient, you can cause permanent injury if you're too aggressive.
- Don't bounce your baby vigorously. This could cause serious head and neck injuries or even death.
- Don't tickle your baby too much or too hard. This is torture.
- Don't toss your baby in the air. You might hurt her neck—or miss catching her.
- Don't pull your baby up by the arms or swing her around. You may dislocate her shoulder or injure her elbow.
- Enjoy your baby and have fun with her.

Caution: Make sure that every person who interacts with your baby understands the dangers of vigorous play.

32. Let Daddy Do It! Ways to Help Dad Enjoy His Baby

- If you haven't had your baby yet, let the expectant Dad help select a name for your baby. Naming your baby is important to him, so find a name that suits you both.

- Let Dad spend time with your baby immediately after the birth. The more time he spends with your baby, the more comfortable and competent he'll feel about baby care.

- If you're breastfeeding, let Dad do other duties, such as bathing, to make up for the time you spend exclusively with your baby.

- Let Dad share equally in bottle-feeding. Often a baby won't take a bottle from a mother who's breastfeeding, so Dad can have this opportunity to spend intimate time with your baby.

- Let Dad have a regular turn changing your baby's diaper. It's a great opportunity to nurture their bond through physical contact.

- Take plenty of pictures of Dad holding your baby.

- Let Dad take care of your baby while you catch up on errands or meet friends for lunch. The more time he spends with your baby, the more attached they'll be.

33. Quick Tip: Fear Factor

I was a little nervous about holding my baby daughter when I first saw her. She was so little, and I was afraid I might hurt her. The nurse at the hospital seemed to sense this. When she brought our baby into the room, she headed right for me and handed me my daughter. It was like diving into the deep end—sink or swim. I stood there frozen for a few seconds, holding her like she was a lobster. And then she looked back at me and I just melted. It didn't take long to realize I wasn't going to hurt her, and now I love holding her.

—*Josh L.*

34. Quick Tip: Daddy Time

I found I needed a break at the end of each day, right about the time my husband got home. My baby seemed to sense this, too, and would start fussing and crying. As soon as my husband walked in the door, I passed the baby to him and took a little break. It was great for all of us, especially my husband, who was eager to see his baby. Of course, our baby was wild about him after spending the entire day with me.

—*Jennifer R.*

35. Quick Tip: Daddy's Day

My husband was a little nervous around our baby, so I made plans with friends and left him in charge for a whole day. It really built his confidence. He learned our baby wasn't as fragile as he thought, and he discovered he could take care of her just as well as I could. Of course, the diaper was on backward when I got home, but I never mentioned that.

—Gina L.

36. Quick Tip: Different Styles

My husband interacted with our baby differently from me. I was really gentle with her, held her close, rocked her a lot, and talked to her a lot. My husband held her less gently—kind of like a football at times—or across his knees. He didn't talk to her as much, but he made lots of funny faces. She seemed to laugh more with him, which was fine with me. I think we complemented each other well.

—Kristin L.

37. Quick Tip: "Daddy!"

Practice teaching your baby the word daddy, *since it's probably going to be her first word. "Da-da" is easier to say than "ma-ma." Your partner will be delighted to hear your baby say his name, and it'll enhance the bond between them.*

—Barbara S.

38. Preparing a Sibling for a New Baby

If you have another child, especially a toddler, you should prepare for some sibling rivalry. There are several ways to help prepare your older child to accept the new baby with minimal jealousy.

Explain what's happening. While you're pregnant, explain to your child what's happening as your baby grows inside you.

Read books. Get some picture books from the library or bookstore and read stories about being an older brother or sister.

Take a class. Take your child to a siblings' class at the local hospital or birth center, so she can learn how to deal with her emotions, help care for your baby, and have fun pretending to be a parent.

Play doctor. Let your child press her ear or hands to your abdomen and feel your baby's movements. Take her to a prenatal checkup (if your doctor allows it), so she can hear the heartbeat or see your baby during an ultrasound.

Talk to your child. Chat with your child about how the new baby will fit into the family. Let your older child know what his or her role will be—and how exciting it will be. Tell your older child how lucky the new baby will be to have him or her as an older brother or sister.

39. Preventing Sibling Rivalry

Once the baby comes, you'll want to include the older sibling as much as possible in baby care and nurturing. The more she feels part of the action, the more smoothly the adjustment will go.

Talk up the "big kid." While nursing or changing your baby, talk about your older child (so she can hear) and brag about how great it is to be a "big kid."

Let your older child help. Teach your older child how to care for your baby—under your careful supervision—and praise her for helping you. Reinforce all the good things she does for the baby. Don't overreact to mishaps.

Do special things with your older child. Have your partner or relative watch your baby while you spend time alone with your older child. Go on a picnic, head to the park, take in a movie, play a game, or do whatever your older child wants to do.

Have your older child do "big kid" stuff. Get your older child involved in "big kid" activities to show her how great it is to grow up. Learning new skills will help her feel competent and confident.

Be honest. Don't promise your older child that life will be the same when the new baby arrives. It won't—no matter how hard you try.

Encourage visitors to pay equal attention to your older child. If someone is bringing a gift for your new baby, ask them to bring one for your older child, too.

Don't worry if your older child regresses a little. Preschool-aged siblings sometimes express a need for attention by acting like the new baby. To counteract this, give them the attention they need and praise them when they act grown-up.

40. Quick Tip: Special Surprise

When a new baby arrives, people can sometimes be insensitive to older siblings without even realizing it. I had some well-meaning friends who liked to visit after I had my second baby. They brought gifts for the baby but nothing for my four-year-old, who cared a lot more about presents than the baby did. I finally bought a few presents for her and hid them. Whenever friends brought gifts for the baby, I gave my older daughter one of the secret gifts signed "From your baby sister." Not only did my four-year-old feel included, she loved getting gifts from her baby sister.
—Joanne M.

41. Soothing Sibling Rivalry

Your child will probably experience some jealousy no matter what you do. It's a natural reaction when a child feels displaced in the family.

Let your older child express her feelings. Even if they're negative, your child's feelings are valid. Talking about them helps her deal with them. Avoid suggesting that her feelings don't exist.

Empathize with your older child. You may have felt the same way when you were a kid, so let her know that you've been there and that her feelings are normal.

Redirect her attention. Give your older child a special task that will remind her that she's an important part of the family.

Place strict limits on aggressive behavior. Make sure your older child understands what is and isn't appropriate around the baby.

Provide healthy ways for her to vent her feelings. For example, give her a doll to play with. If she vents her emotions on the doll, she's less likely to do so on the baby.

Don't compare your children with each other. Avoid establishing a competitive situation by saying something like, "Your brother can do it. Why can't you?" Children are unique individuals with special needs that require noncomparative responses.

42. Quick Tip: Little Mother

My three-year-old was really curious about the baby while I was pregnant. So to help her understand, we played "Make-Believe Mother." I got her a baby doll, diapers, doll clothes, a bassinet, and even a little highchair and baby bathtub. We acted out different scenes every day. She learned so much by being the little mother that by the time the baby came, she was practically giving me advice! We still feed and bathe our babies together.

—Stephanie C.

43. Say Hi to Fluffy and Spot: Preparing the Pets

Sibling rivalry doesn't happen only between children. Sometimes pets feel jealous about a new baby, and they may deliberately misbehave to communicate their frustration.

Prepare the pet. Introduce your pet to the idea of the new baby by showing him the baby's room, equipment, clothing, and so on. Let him spend time in the baby's room so he doesn't feel excluded.

Invite a friend over. If your pet has not shown any signs of aggression toward babies or other children, invite a friend to bring her baby over so your pet can get used to having a baby around.

Meet and greet. Let your pet spend a few minutes getting used to your baby when you first bring her home. Keep your pet calm by petting him and talking to him while he sniffs your baby.

Stand sentry. Keep an eye on your pet at all times when he's around your baby. Never leave them alone together—even if you trust your animal. Pets are unpredictable and need supervision around babies.

Change bad behavior. If your pet displays any unacceptable behaviors around your baby, such as jumping into the baby bed or barking at night, work on changing the behavior immediately. You might want to consult a pet trainer.

Pet problems. If your pet is not accepting the baby and his behavior is getting worse, you might consider keeping him outside or placing him in another home. It's not worth the risk to your baby.

Bonus tip: To help your pet get used to your baby's smell, let him play with a hospital blanket that was used to swaddle your baby.

44. Quick Tip: Baby Your Pet

We had a lot of trouble with our dog after we brought our baby home, even though we thought we had prepared him. I eventually figured out that Scruffy was acting like a spoiled child. He was feeling displaced from the lack of attention that had been transferred to the baby. Once we realized this, we started giving him extra attention, as if he were an older sibling. It worked wonders.

—Connie P.

45. Visiting Hours: Preparing for Family and Friends

During the first few weeks after delivery, you may feel eager to show off your adorable baby to all your relatives and friends. However, the thought of cleaning your home, preparing food, and dressing for company may be overwhelming. You'll still be recovering from the delivery, and you may feel tired and emotional.

Time it right. Limit your guests' visits to once a day (or less), and have people over at your—and your baby's—best time.

Less is more. Limit the number of guests at each visit so you don't feel like you're throwing a party.

Make a date. Encourage people to call and make appointments so you'll be prepared for each visit. Screen your calls and have someone return messages if you're not up to talking.

Lower your standards. Don't feel pressured to clean your home for company. Visitors should understand the mess. (Take out the vacuum cleaner if you want them to think you were just about to clean!)

Keep it simple. Don't make a lot of food. This only encourages guests to stay longer. If you feel the need to serve something, go with simple snacks such as chips, cookies, soda, and so on.

Just say no. If you don't want company, tell your callers you're under doctor's orders to avoid visitors. Hang a sign on the door that reads "Do Not Disturb."

46. Quick Tip: Blame the Doc

I had trouble with my mother-in-law dropping by all the time. She'd try to tell me how to care for my baby and give me advice I didn't want. Rather than risk hurting her feelings, I told her that my doctor said I couldn't have visitors for a while because of high blood pressure. It wasn't too far from the truth. She left me alone for the next couple of weeks, which was heavenly.

—Holly K.

47. What to Do after the Visitors Arrive

If you can't keep family and friends away, here's how to handle them once they've made it through the door.

Short and sweet. Ask your guests to keep their visits short since you have to "feed the baby," "get the baby to sleep," and so on. If your guests outstay their welcome, have a helper step in and insist that you take a break.

Handle with care. If your baby gets fussy while someone is holding her, remove your baby and tell the person he or she can have another try next time.

Prohibit smoking. Tell your visitors not to smoke around your baby, and ask smokers to wash their hands before holding your baby. Nicotine can be transmitted from a smoker's hand to your baby's skin, which can be unhealthy. Also, exposing your baby to secondhand smoke may result in ear and respiratory infections.

48. Quick Tip: No Smoking!

My mother was visiting after I had my baby, and she was a heavy smoker at the time. She followed me into the bedroom as I went in to change my son's diaper. The minute his penis hit the air, he peed in an arc and took out the tip of Mom's cigarette. She didn't jump or move a muscle. She just smiled and said, "I guess he doesn't want me to smoke."
—*Rena L.*

49. Quick Tip:
Thanks for Coming

Some of my visitors offered to help me with chores and things, but I didn't have the courage to accept their generosity. After all, they came to see the baby, not to do my housework. My sister had a great idea. She wrote a note and put it on the refrigerator for everyone to see. "If you want to help the new mother while you're visiting, here's a list: load dishwasher, fold laundry, vacuum, dust, organize baby stuff. Thanks!" It worked great.

—Simonie W.

Chapter 3:
Baby Care Basics

50. Body Building: Baby's Weight and Height

There's a wide range of "normal" in the area of physical development.

Weight. If your baby is full-term, she'll weigh between six and nine pounds. If she's under five and a half pounds, she may be considered low-birth-weight and may need extra support from the hospital team. Visit your baby as much as you can to facilitate the bonding process.

Weight loss. Your baby will lose several ounces (possibly up to ten percent of her birth weight) and gain it back in a week or two. This is normal.

Weight gain. If you're concerned about your baby's weight, check to see that she's producing ten to twelve wet diapers a day and regular, frequent bowel movements, to make sure she's getting enough liquid and nutrition. Breastfed babies should produce a stool a few times a day (once mother's milk is in) and may do so with every nursing.

Length. Almost all babies measure between eighteen and twenty-two inches in length, even slightly premature babies. Your baby's adult height depends primarily on heredity. If you provide her with good nutrition, she'll most likely reach her genetically predetermined height.

51. Infant Massage

Give your baby a massage every day. Massage greatly improves digestion and bonding. Massage can help develop your baby's senses, too. Use gentle circular movements or long-stroking movements. You want to move the blood *toward* your baby's heart, so start at the fingers and move slowly up your baby's arm. It's best to have warm hands and maintain skin-to-skin contact. Look your baby in the eyes when you're massaging her back.

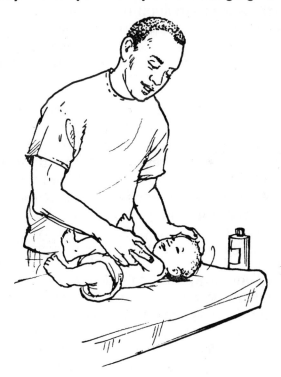

52. This Side Up: Your Baby's Head

If you get a chance to see your baby during delivery, you'll most likely see his head before the rest of his body pops out. In fact, he may look like he's all head when he's first born.

Size. A baby's head is large in proportion to the rest of his body. A newborn's head measures one-fourth of his body length, whereas an adult head measures one-eighth. A baby's body catches up with his head by the time he reaches adulthood. Keep your baby's head covered after birth, especially if it's chilly outside, since he can lose heat quickly through his head.

Shape. If your baby's head is slightly cone-shaped at birth, don't worry; it's temporary. The skull is pliable at birth, allowing the head bones to overlap when traveling through the birth canal. Pressure from the trip may cause the head to flatten, but it usually rounds out in a day or two. If your baby spends a lot of time on his back, however, his head may flatten at the back. To prevent this, make sure he gets plenty of tummy time while awake. If you're concerned, talk to your doctor.

Soft spots. Your baby has two soft spots, or fontanels, on his head: one on the top (center) and the other in the back (center). The soft spot at the back closes up in the first months, while the one on top closes up after the first year. You can feel your baby's pulse through the soft spot. Don't be afraid to touch it gently; it won't cave in.

Marks and bumps. If your baby was delivered with forceps, he may have some bruises on the sides of his head. These marks should clear up in a few days. If he was delivered with a vacuum extractor, he may have a lump on the top of his head. This should also disappear in a few days. Even though your baby's head is somewhat resilient, be careful not to bump it or jar it.

Hair. Some babies have lots of hair on their head when they're born; others are nearly bald. Babies lose some hair in the first few weeks, but it eventually grows back, sometimes in a different color.

Cradle cap. Cradle cap refers to the dry, flaky, or scaly skin on the top of a newborn's head. It often disappears on its own in the first months. Washing, combing, and brushing the scales may help the scalp look better, but the condition usually doesn't bother the baby. If the crusts are especially thick and accompanied by a red scaly rash in the skin creases, talk to your doctor about possible treatments.

53. Quick Tip: Cradle Cap

When my baby's head started flaking from cradle cap (I called it cradle crap), I put a little baby oil on her head and gently massaged it in. She didn't care how she looked, of course, but it made me feel better. I also clipped a little ribbon to the fuzz on top of her head (she had no hair yet), because everyone kept calling her a boy.

—Rena L.

54. Handy Facts: Arms, Hands, and Fingers

Arms. Your baby's arms may look thin and scrawny or fat and pudgy, depending on her birth weight and body type. Early on, she doesn't have much control over her arm movements, but that will come soon after she gets control over her trunk. Control moves down the arm to the hands and fingers. Arm movements are considered gross motor, while hand and finger movements are called fine motor. Your baby's arms are usually flexed most of the time. Help relax them by gently opening and closing them, rotating them in circles, moving them up and down, and waving them from side to side.

Hands. Your baby's hands are usually tightfisted early on, and the fingers have to be gently uncurled. Your baby has a tight grasp and often can't let go because of her reflexes. Her eye-hand coordination begins developing at birth as she tries to reach out and make contact with what she sees. Help her practice uncurling and spreading her fingers, then allow her to wrap her hand around your fingers again.

Fingers. Your baby likes to put her fingers in her mouth to comfort herself and explore her hands. Let her suck on her thumb, fingers, even her fist if she wants to.

Pincer grasp. Your baby's pincer grasp (using the thumb and forefinger together) will develop around nine to twelve months. Have her practice her pincer grasp by giving her small bits of food to pick up and put in her mouth. Keep an eye on her, though, since she'll want to pick up all kinds of objects and put those in her mouth, too.

Fingernails. Your baby's fingernails start growing in the womb, so she's likely to have nails when she's born. Since she has a tendency to grasp and scratch her face, trim her nails with baby scissors or keep her hands covered, especially while she's sleeping.

Freedom of movement. Babies are often swaddled after birth. This warms them, comforts them, and helps ease the transition from the womb. As your baby gets older, give her more freedom to move her arms and hands. She'll make faster gains in all areas of development if she can move her limbs and explore her fingers.

55. Quick Tip: Dealing with Fingernails

When my baby's fingernails got long, I tried cutting them with baby scissors, but she hated that. I even tried cutting them while she was asleep, but almost everything woke her up. Finally I gently peeled the tips off. The nails are really soft and the tips are easy to peel. Sometimes I put her fingers in my mouth and bit the nails off, which she actually liked.
—Vicki S.

56. The Bottom Half: Legs, Feet, and Toes

Your baby's legs develop the same way his arms do. He gains control over his legs first, then his feet, then his toes (but not to the same extent as his hands and fingers).

Legs. Your baby may appear bowlegged when he's born. His legs have been curled up for months in the womb, but they'll straighten out over the first two years of life. Your doctor will check the hip sockets after birth to make sure nothing is out of alignment. Let your baby stand up and exercise his legs all he wants. It's good for him.

Feet. Your baby's feet are also curled at birth. Stroke the bottoms of his feet, and his toes will curl in. Stroke the sides of his feet, and his toes will spread. To help him straighten his feet, hold him upright and place his feet on a flat surface. Watch him try to stand and step.

Toes. Your baby's toes are curled under at birth but will eventually straighten out. Uncurl his toes gently as you massage his feet. Trim his toenails with baby scissors as needed.

Shoes. Shoes aren't necessary for baby's development. In fact, they serve mainly as decoration in the early months. It's best to let your child be barefoot as much as possible so he can practice his gross motor skills. If you want him to wear shoes occasionally, make sure they're flexible, not rigid.

57. Quick Tip: No Shoes

*My baby started walking at ten months, so I thought it
was time to buy him some shoes. As soon as I put them on
his feet, he had trouble managing them. They really
seemed to interfere with his steps. So I took them off.
Having his feet free seemed to give him more stability. It
was too bad, because the shoes were really cute and I paid
a lot for them. By the time I tried to put them back on his
feet, he'd outgrown them. I saved them anyway.*

—Jennifer R.

58. Baby's Reflexes

Babies are born with several survival reflexes that help them adjust to life outside the womb. Many of these reflexes (such as grasping) disappear over time, while others stay with them for life (such as breathing).

Breathing. The breathing reflex begins the moment your baby's head and chest are out of the womb. After she expands her lungs and takes her first breath, your baby will hiccup, sneeze, and gasp from time to time—all normal glitches in the breathing process. In the early weeks, a baby's breathing has some normal irregularity and fluctuation (called periodic breathing). However, if you think your baby's breathing is labored or if there are long lapses between breaths, call your doctor.

Startle. If you make a loud noise or move your baby suddenly, she'll startle (throw her arms and legs out, recoil them, and cry). Experts believe this Moro reflex helps babies hold on to their mothers in times of stress. Avoid loud noises and sudden movements. If you startle your baby accidentally, soothe her until she feels secure again.

Palmar grasp. If you stroke your baby's palm, she'll wrap her fingers around your finger with a grasp so strong it's difficult for her to release. If your baby grasps your hair or another object you don't want her to hold, unpeel her fingers slowly and carefully. Don't try to pull the object forcefully out of her hands.

Crying. Your baby's cries begin as a reflex. As time goes on, she cries to communicate her various needs. Feel free to pick her up and soothe her when she cries, no matter what your friends and relatives might say. She may be lonely and needing your attention.

59. Quick Tip: Startling Cry

It seemed like every time I said something to my baby or moved him, he startled. He'd throw his arms and legs out and burst into tears. He was so sensitive. I felt bad, as if I were really scaring him. I started talking softly and moving slowly, and he startled a lot less. He also seemed calmer throughout the day. I think being sensitive to your baby in the first few weeks helps him get used to all the new sounds and movements.

—Kelly V.

60. Quick Tip: Distinguishing Cries

In the beginning, I could never tell my baby's cries apart. I felt really bad about it. I had two friends who could tell when their babies were wet or hungry or tired, just by their cries. Finally, I wrote down all the reasons why my baby might be crying. Each time my baby started crying, I went down the list until I found the solution. After about a month or so, I started to hear the differences in her cries. But I never forgot how frustrating it was in those first few weeks.

—Melissa A.

61. Reflexes versus Voluntary Movement

Many reflexes lead to voluntary movements over time. The stepping reflex is a precursor to walking, the grasping reflex changes from automatic to deliberate, and as the rooting reflex gradually disappears, sucking and swallowing eventually come under a baby's control.

Reach and grasp. Give your baby practice reaching and grasping by moving a toy in front of him near his hands and within his grasp. Put him on the floor and set a toy near his hand so he has the opportunity to reach for it. Make sure it's close enough to grasp. Babies can usually do this around three to four months.

Tonic neck reflex. Lay your baby on his back and turn his head to one side. Watch one arm and leg draw up while the other two stretch out. Gently turn your baby's head in the opposite direction and watch his arms and legs reverse position. This reflex is most prominent at two months and disappears around four to five months.

Stepping and walking reflex. Let your baby stretch out his legs, support his weight, and take little steps on a flat surface. These reflexes will disappear after the first months and return as deliberate movements around nine to twelve months.

62. Quick Tip: Hair Puller

My baby had a really strong grasp that she couldn't release easily. She'd occasionally grab my hair and really pull it, especially while nursing. It hurt, and I lost quite a few hairs that way. I finally learned to tie my hair back before I nursed her, and she learned to grab my collar instead. Then I started giving her small toys to hold on to, since she always seemed to want to hold something while she nursed.
—Holly K.

63. Quick Tip: Baby Book

I collected all the memorabilia after my baby was born: the hospital bracelet, flower petals, cards, photos, everything. At night while my husband held the baby, I worked on her baby book. Each week I added something new I'd saved, such as the label from her first jar of baby food, her doctor appointment card, the wrapper from her favorite toy, even her first T-shirt she outgrew in record time.
—Mary W.

64. See the Light: Baby's Vision

Experts once thought that babies' senses were poorly developed at birth. Now we know that babies are much more sensitive than we realized. Evidence indicates that babies can distinguish between light and dark in the womb. After birth, they have trouble seeing objects farther away than thirty inches, but most babies focus fairly well when you hold an object about eight to twelve inches from their face. By two years of age, your baby's sight will have improved from 20/400 to 20/60. Color vision seems to be absent at birth, but it becomes apparent by two to three months. Your baby may be able to distinguish among red, green, and white at first, adding new colors as her color perception expands.

Visual toys. Provide your baby with toys that offer plenty of visual stimulation, such as bright busy boxes, moving mobiles, and colorful crib toys.

Moving objects. Beginning at a few weeks to one month, hold an interesting toy about eight to twelve inches from your baby's face. Move it slowly from side to side, then up and down. Watch your baby's eyes try to follow it. Do this every day and watch how her visual tracking improves.

Items around your home. Walk around your home showing your baby all the interesting things to look at. Babies begin learning through visual stimulation; so the more she sees, the faster she'll learn.

A room with a view. Put up pictures of babies, animals, bright colorful objects, and other interesting objects on the walls, doors, and ceiling of your baby's room. Hang stuffed animals on a clothesline across the room, and put up lots of posters and wall hangings for her to look at.

Preferences. Babies prefer to look at certain visual objects, so provide the following for your baby to study and enjoy:
- Human faces
- Interesting patterns rather than solids
- Contrasts, especially black and white
- Moving objects rather than still ones
- Complex objects rather than simple ones
- New images rather than old ones
- Three-dimensional objects rather than two-dimensional ones

65. Listen Up: Baby's Hearing

Your baby's hearing is well developed at birth. Watch him carefully and you may notice how he responds differently to various noises.

Pitch. Babies prefer high-pitched voices to low-pitched ones, so women's voices are usually more attractive than men's. Speak to your baby in a high-pitched voice to get him to listen to you. Men often do this intuitively, as if they have a sixth sense that babies prefer a high-pitched voice.

Parents' voices. Your newborn can distinguish your voice from other voices because he hears it in the womb and recognizes it after birth. Talk to your baby frequently before and after birth, so he can become very familiar with your voice.

Basic responses. If you want your baby to fall asleep, turn on white noise such as the vacuum cleaner or dryer. Avoid sudden loud noises, so you don't startle him.

Speech sounds. By one month your baby is already absorbing the speech sounds he will eventually make. He can also perceive differences among speech sounds. Speak to him often, using simple words and phrases. The more you speak to him, the more he'll learn. His vocabulary will develop rapidly, and he'll probably say his first word by the end of the first year.

Music. Your baby may respond to music in various ways: by sleeping, kicking his legs, waving his arms, or moving rhythmically. Babies can differentiate a variety of tempos and sounds. Play different kinds of music to stimulate your baby's auditory development.

Quiet. Most babies tune out the world quite effectively, so you usually don't need absolute silence while your baby is sleeping. However, if your baby is very sensitive to sounds, put him in a quiet place to sleep.

66. Quick Tip: Voice-Over

I read to my baby every night. She really seemed to like hearing my voice. One time we had a long ride ahead of us, so the night before I taped myself reading her a story. I played the tape in the car while I concentrated on driving. She was entertained the whole trip. My older son also used the tape and followed along with the book. Over and over and over....

—Holly K.

67. Hearing Concerns

Most babies are tested at birth for deafness. Check to see if your baby has had this newborn hearing test. Early intervention can make a difference in dealing with hearing problems.

Chronic serous otitis media, or otitis media with effusion, is a condition that usually appears as a complication of a middle-ear infection. The middle ear becomes filled with fluid that can cause temporary hearing loss. This may impair speech and language development, and needs to be followed by a doctor. Here are some signs that your baby may have an ear infection:

- Crying and fussing for long periods of time
- Rubbing her ear or the side of her face
- Not responding to your voice or other soft sounds
- Having a stuffy or runny nose
- Coughing
- Generally not feeling well

68. Feeling Fine: Baby's Sense of Touch

Although your baby will recoil from a painful stimulus, she'll respond positively to your gentle, soothing touch.

Contact. Hold your baby as much as you like. She'll make rapid gains in all areas of development if she's handled, caressed, and touched often.

Massage. Massage is one of the most effective ways of soothing a fussy baby. (See page 43.) Feel free to massage her when she's happy, too.

Mouth. Your baby learns about objects by putting them in her mouth. Allow her to explore safe objects (such as pacifiers) orally, so she can begin to learn about texture, size, weight, hardness, and temperature.

69. Quick Tip: Prevent Choking

My baby choked on a small toy that I thought was safe for him. He managed to get it stuck in his mouth, and luckily I was able to get it out. It really freaked us out, though. When I told my doctor, he recommended a gizmo that tests small objects for safety. If you can fit the object in the gizmo, it's not safe around your baby. I found it at the baby store (very inexpensive), and I take it with me wherever I go.

—Chris S.

70. Take a Breath: Baby's Sense of Smell

A newborn's sense of smell is very acute. As your baby learns where various smells come from, he begins to recognize them and respond to them in different ways. For example, a breastfed baby can tell his mother's smell from other people's smells, including other nursing women and Dad. If Dad has trouble bottle-feeding your baby when you're not available to breastfeed, have Dad wear your robe or shirt. Your smell on the robe or shirt may fool your baby into thinking his mother is holding him, and he may then take the bottle.

71. Quick Tip: Baby Poster

Put up a poster of a baby over the crib so your baby can look at it while she's lying in bed. Babies are really attracted to other babies, and my daughter just loved it. I wish I would have made a poster enlargement of her photograph,

but I didn't think of it until she was older. Now she keeps a poster of herself over her bed so she can say good night to herself before she goes to sleep.

—Joanne M.

72. Tickle the Tongue: Baby's Sense of Taste

A baby's sense of taste is not well developed at birth, but it does exist.

Preference. Although your baby can distinguish among sour, salty, and bitter tastes, he prefers sweet tastes such as breastmilk. When you begin to introduce solids, you may want to start with cereals or vegetables; once your baby has tasted the sweetness of fruits, he may be less interested in other tastes.

Solid food. Many pediatricians recommend introducing solid foods around four to six months. Some babies are ready for solids earlier than others. Some experts believe that a baby's sense of taste peaks at one year, so that may be a good time to introduce lots of new flavors.

Tongue thrust. Some parents think babies stick out their tongues during feedings because they don't like the taste of something. Actually, babies have a tongue thrust reflex that causes them to push out their tongues when something is placed in their mouths. Look at your baby's face to learn whether he likes something or not, and keep a positive look on your face while you feed him.

73. Here's the Skinny: Baby's Skin

The first thing you may notice about your baby's skin is how soft and smooth it is. You'll notice other things as you get better acquainted.

Vernix. The coating on your baby's skin at birth is known as vernix caseosa. It's a white creamy substance that protects your baby's skin while she's in the womb. After she's born, gently rub the vernix into your baby's skin to protect it from flaking.

Stork bites. These small, reddish-pink marks on your baby's skin are tiny broken capillaries that will disappear over time. They're commonly located at the nape of the neck. You don't need to worry about them.

Jaundice. If your baby's skin has a yellowish tint, she may have newborn jaundice. It's normal for a baby to have a mild degree of jaundice. It means her liver is not quite fully functioning after birth. Call your doctor if you notice a significant degree of tint. Your doctor may place your baby under bilirubin lights or wrap her in a special bilirubin blanket, which should correct the problem easily and safely within a day or two.

Lanugo. Some babies born prematurely exhibit a coating of fine downy hair that covers them inside the uterus. Lanugo usually disappears by the time a full-term baby is ready to be born. There's no need to shave it off; it will disappear on its own.

Milia. These are tiny, flat, white or yellow bumps on a newborn's nose. They're normal and go away in the first few weeks.

Infant acne. A week or two after your baby is born, she may look like she's developed acne. This is usually related to hormones and will often disappear over the first few weeks or months. If the acne is severe, talk to your doctor.

Bathing. There's no need for special soaps, lotions, or powders on your baby's skin. In fact, some of these products can be harmful. Just wash your baby every other day with mild soap and water. That's all she needs in the way of skin care. Dry, scaly skin is common in the first few days and will usually normalize on its own.

74. Crybaby: Your Baby's First Language

Your baby tries to make it easy for you to take care of him (although it may not seem that way). He cries to let you know he's hungry, wet, lonely, bored, tired, and so on. Early on those cries may sound the same, but over time you may learn to distinguish your baby's different cries so you can satisfy his needs more quickly.

Wet or dirty. When your baby needs a diaper change, he'll usually fuss or cry gently—his way of sharing his discomfort. Check his diaper and make a change, if necessary. That may be the end of the crying for a while.

Hungry. Your baby's hunger cry is usually more vigorous. After you've checked his diaper, see if he wants to nurse. Give him the breast or bottle to quiet him down and satisfy those hunger pangs.

Lonely. If your baby needs to be held, he may fuss or cry loudly. If you've checked his diaper and tried feeding him, perhaps he just wants to be comforted. His need for human contact and companionship is just as strong as his need for food. Try putting him in your front pack or sling while doing your chores.

Needing to suck. If your baby has been fed but seems to need more sucking time, help him find his thumb, provide him with a pacifier, or let him suck on the underside of your finger. Most babies have an intense need to suck—for comfort, security, and to help calm themselves.

Bored. If your baby is still fussing after being fed and changed and held, he might be bored. Place him in your lap, prop him up with your knees, and play with him. Sing songs, talk to him, or entertain him with a toy.

Tired. If you've tried everything else and your baby is still crying, he might be tired, overwhelmed, or overstimulated. Place him in his crib, rock him, try the baby swing, or take him for a ride.

75. Quick Tip: Teatime

My baby had gas problems and a crampy tummy, so I used fennel tea to settle her stomach. I recommended this to several friends, and they all said it worked. The recipe is 2–3 tablespoons fennel seeds, 1–2 tablespoons Karo syrup, and 1 cup water. Boil the seeds and water for 30 minutes until the water is almost the color of tea. Add the Karo syrup, let the tea cool to room temperature, strain the seeds, and feed to baby in a bottle. The fennel seems to stop the gas, and it has a generally soothing effect on babies.
—Cindy M.

76. Bellybutton Business: Umbilical Cord Care

Since there's no pain sensitivity in the umbilical cord, cutting and clamping the cord do not hurt your baby. Monitor the cord stump with care until it falls off.

Color. Within an average of ten to fourteen days, your baby's cord stump will turn dark, dry up, and fall off on its own. Don't be concerned about the color; this is normal.

Cleaning. Reduce the risk of infection by keeping the cord area dry while the stump is still attached. Keep the diaper away from the cord area by folding it over or under. Give your baby a sponge bath until the stump falls off.

Care. Swab a little isopropyl alcohol on the cord stump to help dry it out and keep it from getting infected.

Concern. If your baby's cord seems infected (red, hot, painful, puffy, or oozy), call your doctor. It's normal for the cord to have some odor and drainage, especially right before it falls off.

In or out? Contrary to certain myths, there's no way to influence whether your baby will have an "inny" or an "outy." Bellybutton style is genetically determined. It has nothing to do with where the cord is cut.

77. Genitals/Circumcision Care

Your baby's genitals may be swollen in the first hours and days after birth, as a result of maternal hormones still circulating through his body. Use warm water and a warm washcloth (and maybe a little mild soap) to clean them. Change your baby's diaper frequently to keep the area as dry as possible, especially if your baby's penis has been circumcised.

Attitudes toward circumcision are changing. Not long ago it was a routine procedure seldom discussed by parents and doctors. Now the decision is much more carefully considered. The most common reasons to circumcise are cultural, religious, aesthetic, and because the father wants his son to look like him. Although some studies suggest that circumcision might reduce the risk of penile cancer, sexually transmitted diseases, and urinary tract infections, more research is needed. If you choose to have your baby circumcised, it's best to have it done before your son leaves the hospital or in the first weeks after birth.

Care. Give your baby a sponge bath until the circumcision heals, usually within a few days to a week. Be careful with your son's penis during the first few days after circumcision; it will be tender and sore.

Medication. Use a protective gel or ointment to help protect the penis from the diaper while it's healing.

Concerns. Watch for bleeding and signs of infection. Call your doctor if the penis oozes, swells, gets hot, turns red, seems painful, or doesn't look like it's healing.

78. Chew On This: Teething

Babies begin teething at around six months. They often show signs of teething weeks and even months before teeth actually appear. Common signs include irritability, drooling, chafed lips, frequent chewing of toys or fingers, swollen gums, diarrhea, mild fever, ear pulling, and loss of appetite.

Patterns. Baby teeth usually appear in pairs, with the lower front incisors usually appearing first. The other six incisors (four on top and two more on the bottom) usually appear between six and twelve months.

Timing. Pairs of baby teeth, or sometimes four at a time, usually appear every four months or so. Girls usually get their teeth before boys. Lower teeth usually appear before upper teeth, with the uppers following shortly after the lower ones. Some tendencies to cut teeth earlier or later appear to be genetic.

Molars. The first molars appear sometime between twelve and eighteen months.

Canines. The canine teeth, located in front of the first molars, usually appear between eighteen and twenty-four months.

Two-year molars. The second set of molars, located behind the first set, usually appear between twenty-four and thirty months.

79. Toothaches: Dealing with Teething Discomfort

Drool. Drool can cause a drippy nose and looser-than-normal stools, and it may be confused with an ear infection.

Rash. Drooling sometimes causes a rash around a baby's mouth. Wipe off the drool gently with a soft cloth, and use a mild non-allergenic lotion around the area.

Sensitivity. Many babies feel only a sensitivity on their gums, which causes minor fussing. Other babies feel real pain and cry.

Fever. Some babies develop a low-grade fever while they're teething. If your baby has a slight fever, give him acetaminophen according to doctor's instructions.

Bite. Babies like to bite on cold or hard objects while they're teething. Your baby may enjoy gnawing on your fingers and thumb as you rub his gums.

Teethers. Offer your baby a frozen teether, Popsicle, washcloth wrapped around ice cubes, or teething biscuits.

Caution: Sucking may actually aggravate the pain, since it brings blood to the gums instead of pushing it away. Encourage your baby to chew rather than suck while he's teething. Instead of using a pacifier, give him something larger, such as a teething ring, to encourage chewing rather than sucking.

80. Baby Toothbrush: Baby Dental Care

When your baby finally gets her teeth, it's time to start brushing.

Toothbrush. Begin cleaning your baby's teeth with a soft baby toothbrush that's brightly colored or decorated with cartoon characters.

Training. Early brushing helps your baby learn the importance of dental hygiene. Get her in the habit from the start.

Treats. Monitor the intake of sugary foods and drinks (such as cupcakes and fruit juice) that may stick to the teeth and cause decay. Wipe your baby's teeth or gently brush them after giving sugary foods. Also, don't allow your baby to fall asleep with a milk bottle. Milk can pool around the teeth and cause decay.

81. Quick Tip: Brushing Model

My baby was fascinated with the toothbrush. He followed my every move while I brushed my teeth. I finally gave him his own toothbrush to chew on, and he loved it. I had to be careful that he didn't try to stick it down his throat, though. When it came time for him to brush, he was already way ahead of the game.

—*Rosio S.*

Chapter 4:
Diapering

82. Diaper Duty

When you mention diapers to most people, you usually get a funny face in response. Diaper changing doesn't seem to be high on the list of favorite things to do. But as parents of a young baby, you'll be missing a special opportunity if you consider this duty unpleasant. Since there are so many trips to the changing table throughout the day, you can use this time to reinforce your special bond with your baby.

Urination. Although it may seem as if your baby is always wet, most newborns produce six to eight wet diapers a day. This number increases to eight to twelve diapers a day in the following weeks. If your baby is not producing an appropriate number of wet diapers, check with your doctor to make sure he's gaining weight and getting enough milk.

Bowel Movements. Your baby's first stool, called meconium, looks something like black tar. It's usually passed in the first twenty-four hours after birth. After that, the stools become yellowish brown. Formula-fed babies have firmer and less frequent stools than breast-fed babies. Some babies produce bowel movements with every feeding, while others save up for a few days. Both are considered within the range of normal. In breastfed babies, infrequent stools can be a sign of poor feeding. Watch for any changes in your baby's stools, such as extreme wateriness or extreme constipation, and check with your doctor if you have any concerns.

83. Quick Tip:
Quick Diaper Check

Sometimes it's hard to tell if your baby is wet when he's wearing disposable diapers. I hated wasting a diaper when I thought it was time to change him (and it wasn't), but I didn't want to risk a rash by not changing him enough. Then I figured out a quick way to check his diaper. I stuck my finger under the edge of the diaper and felt the pad. I could tell instantly whether it was wet or not. Just don't forget to wash your hands!

—Gina L.

84. Cloth Diapers

You may not realize it, but you'll be changing between five and seven thousand diapers during your baby's first years of life. That's a lot of diaper changing! One of the most important decisions regarding diapers is whether to use cloth or disposables. You need to take into account convenience, cost, cleaning, and disposing of the diapers.

Pros

- Cloth diapers aren't as harmful to the environment, since they can be recycled. You don't have to feel guilty about using them.
- Cloth diapers aren't as expensive as disposables, unless you use a diaper service.
- Cloth diapers don't cause as much diaper rash because you can tell when the diaper is wet, unless the diaper is covered with plastic pants.
- Cloth diapers are more comfortable, unless they're double diapered and overly bulky.

Cons

- Cloth diapers are not as easy to use as disposable diapers, since they require folding and plastic pants (or diaper pins).

- Soiled cloth diapers have to be stored in a container until cleaning time, so you have to deal with the odor.

- Cloth diapers have to be washed or at least prepared for the diaper service.

- Cloth diapers often produce more leakage, unless they're covered with plastic pants. Then the wetness may go unnoticed for longer periods, and the risk of diaper rash may increase.

- Cloth diapers aren't as convenient as disposables when you're traveling with your baby.

Bonus tip: You'll need about two dozen cloth diapers to make sure you always have clean ones ready, unless you plan to wash diapers every day.

Bonus tip: Some cloth diapers have tabs, so you don't have to use diaper pins. If you use a diaper pin, run it along a bar of soap so it slides through the diaper more easily.

85. Disposable Diapers

Pros

- Disposable diapers are easier and more convenient to use.
- They're easier to dispose of.
- They don't have to be folded before you put them on your baby.
- They eliminate the risk of your baby getting pricked with a diaper pin.
- They're easier to use when you're traveling with your baby.

Bonus tip: You might consider using a combination of cloth and disposable diapers, depending on your philosophy, needs, mood, travel schedule, and so on.

Bonus tip: Check your baby's diaper frequently to make sure it isn't wet. The most common cause of diaper rash is urine in the genital area for long periods of time. The drier you keep your baby, the less chance he has of developing a diaper rash.

Cons

- Disposable diapers are harder on the environment, since they're not recyclable.
- They're more expensive than cloth diapers, unless you're using a diaper service.
- They can lead to more rashes, since it's more difficult to tell if your baby is wet.
- They're not as soft and comfortable as cloth diapers.

86. Quick Tip: Torn Tabs

I loved everything about disposable diapers except the tabs. I kept tearing them, which ruined the whole diaper. Eventually I discovered that, instead of throwing the diaper away, I could repair the tab with masking tape. I saved a lot of diapers that way—and a lot of frustration.

—Chris S.

87. Diaper Dealings: Changing Baby's Diaper

Changing your baby's diaper can be a pleasant experience if you approach it with a good attitude and a sense of fun. If you see it as an opportunity to share quality time with your baby through conversation, smiles, and songs, you may actually look forward to it.

Preparation. Before you begin, be sure you have all the supplies on hand so you don't have to leave your baby alone for even a second on the changing table. The moment you take a chance may be the moment she chooses to roll over, perhaps for the first time. This happens all too often.

Convenience. Create a comfortable changing environment. A changing table is best since it contains lots of storage spaces and it places your baby at a convenient height. Lay a waterproof pad on the changing surface to protect it from getting wet.

Smiles. Keep a positive attitude while changing your baby's diaper, so she doesn't sense that you're disgusted by the task. Smiling will also keep her entertained. She's watching you as you work, so concentrate more on your interaction with her and less on the dirty diaper.

Safe disposal. Set the diaper aside or deposit it in the diaper pail while keeping a hand on your baby. Keep a spare diaper handy in case your baby wets the one you're about to use—or if he sprays!

Comfort. After you remove the wet diaper, lay the dry diaper on top of your baby to keep her warm. Use pre-moistened wipes or a fresh wet washcloth to clean the genital area. Always wipe from front to back, never the reverse. Never use a soiled wipe or washcloth.

Cream. Spread a little diaper cream on the genital area if your baby is showing signs of redness. Change her diaper as often as needed to keep the area dry and reduce the chance of diaper rash.

Cloth. If you're using cloth diapers, fold the diaper into thirds, lengthwise. Lift your baby's feet and bottom, and slip the diaper underneath. Spread your baby's legs, and pull the diaper over her genitals to her stomach. Carefully secure the diaper on both sides. If you're using pins, be careful not to prick your baby.

Disposable. If you're using disposable diapers, there's no need to fold them. Just make sure the tabs are on the underside of your baby when positioning the diaper. Tape them toward the front as your secure the diaper. Make sure it isn't too tight.

Double. If you're using cloth diapers, consider double diapering your baby if she has frequent urinations. Double diaper her at night as well, so she'll be protected longer and perhaps sleep longer.

Play. Entertain your baby while you change her diaper. Make it fun for both of you. Keep a special toy handy, turn on the overhead mobile, sing a song, or play some music.

88. The Diaper District: Ready for a Change

After you've selected your changing area, you'll need the following supplies.

- Supply of clean diapers
- Diaper pins or tape
- Diaper rash ointment
- Moistened disposable wipes or washcloths
- Change of clothes
- Toys, mobile, music box
- Diaper pail

Bonus tip: If possible, store baby wipes near a heat vent so they're warm when you need them. Store the container upside down occasionally, to keep all the wipes moist and to prevent the ones at the bottom from getting too soggy.

Caution: There's no need for powder or lotion on your baby's bottom. In fact, powder products may be harmful to your baby if inhaled, or they may cause an allergic reaction.

Caution: Watch out for boys—they like to spray you the moment the diaper's off. Keep your son's penis covered with a fresh diaper while you finish wiping him.

89. Quick Tip: Squirmy Changes

If your baby squirms a lot while you're trying to change his diaper or clothes, tie a toy to your wrist to entertain him while you work. Let it dangle so he can bat at it. If you have a charm bracelet or bracelets that make noise, wear those so he can play with them.

—Cara V.

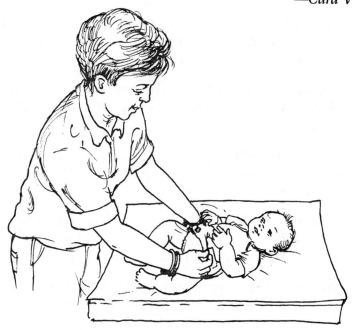

90. Diaper Diversions: Changing Time Is Fun

Each time you change your baby's diaper, be prepared to entertain, amuse, and interact with her. Babies sometimes get wriggly when they have their diapers changed. Keeping them distracted will usually do the trick.

Talk. Chat with your baby about your day, your plans, or your dreams. Give her a chance to "talk back" so you can have a "conversation."

Songs. Even if you're not the greatest singer, don't be afraid to belt out a few songs or lullabies as you change your baby.

Silly sounds. Use your mouth to make raspberries, smacking noises, kisses, motorboats, puffs, snorts, and anything else you can think of.

Tongue ticklers. Entertain your baby with your tongue by wiggling it, sticking it in and out, making clicking sounds, and so on.

Funny faces. Keep your baby smiling by making funny faces to go with the funny noises. Be careful not to frighten your baby with a scary face!

Tummy time fun. Set a toy on your baby's tummy, make funny noises on it, play a game such as Round-and-Round-the-Mountain, and so on.

Games. Play games such as Pat-a-Cake, Peek-a-Boo, Eye Winker, and so on.

Sights to see. Hang a mobile, mirror, or colorful picture over the changing table, so your baby has something interesting to look at.

Toys. Keep a supply of squeaky toys, stuffed animals, and puppets handy to use while changing your baby.

91. Quick Tip: Diaper Dancing

As my baby got older, he refused to lie down for a diaper change no matter what I did to distract and cajole him. I finally gave up and changed his diaper while he remained standing. It worked! He stood still long enough for me to finish. It was a little awkward, but it was worth the effort to avoid a battle.

—Melanie E.

92. Rash Decisions: Preventing and Treating Diaper Rash

Diaper rash is usually caused by frequent or lengthy exposure to urine or bowel movements, a high acid content in urine or stools, overuse of soap, or rubbing too hard. High acid content occurs naturally in some babies, and can be difficult to control. The best way to deal with diaper rash is prevention. If you discover your baby has a rash, it's relatively easy to cure if you attend to it quickly.

Check often. Frequent diaper changing is the best way to prevent diaper rash. Check your baby often and change him at the first sign of wetness.

Watch for stool changes. Some rashes develop as a result of acidic urine or diarrhea, some are caused by teething or food sensitivity, and some are due to illness. Watch for changes in your baby's stools as a sign of impending diaper rash. If the skin around the anus is red and sore, avoid wiping or rubbing the area. Instead, promote healing by soaking any stools off your baby's bottom.

Avoid wipes and soap. Avoid baby wipes if they sting your baby's bottom. Use a warm washcloth and water only. Place the washcloth in the laundry and use a fresh one next time.

Air exposure. Place your baby on a waterproof pad without a diaper for several minutes. You can also increase air exposure by using larger diapers and putting them on a bit looser.

Creams. Use ointments designed for diaper rash at the first sign of redness. If the ointment doesn't clear up the rash in a day or two, call your doctor.

Thorough cleaning. Sometimes the rash hides in the folds of your baby's genital area, and you don't see it unless you check carefully. Use diaper cream inside the folds, but be careful not to get it inside your baby's labia.

Caution: The rash may be caused by an allergy to a diaper product, soap, or ointment you're using. Consider changing products if the rash keeps coming back. Avoid waterproof pants while your baby has a rash.

93. Quick Tip: Rash Decision

My baby was really susceptible to diaper rash. It seemed like every other day he'd have a rash no matter how often or how quickly I changed him. A friend recommended using a little diaper rash cream at every changing to help prevent the problem. So I tried it. It worked. The cream seemed to give him a nice barrier that helped prevent future rashes.

—Stephanie C.

94. Quick Tip: Feeling Free

I highly recommend daily nude time for your baby. My daughter became a different person when I took her diaper off. She loved being naked. It seemed to change her personality. She waved her arms and legs, made funny noises, smiled, and laughed. I let her have nude time every day. I put a large beach towel on the carpet to protect it from accidents.

—Melanie E.

Chapter 5:
Bathing

95. Sponge Bath

Your baby's first baths are usually sponge baths, since you need to keep the cord area dry until the stump falls off (usually ten days to two weeks after the birth). A sponge bath also helps reduce the risk of infection in the circumcision area. (See page 67.) You should probably plan to use sponge baths for one to three weeks after the birth, depending on the circumstances. Talk to your doctor.

Checklist. Prepare a checklist and have everything ready so you don't have to leave your baby or take him out of the bath to retrieve something.

Temperature. Make sure the room temperature is comfortable so your baby doesn't get too cold. You can keep him covered with an extra towel as you clean different parts of his body.

Bathtub. Use a small plastic tub lined with a bath sponge for security. Set up the plastic tub in the kitchen sink or regular bathtub.

Position. Lay your baby in the tub (without water). Hold him firmly (but not too tight!) so he feels secure.

Washing. Wash your baby's face and hair gently with a little water and a washcloth. Then wash his body with mild soap and a wet washcloth. Be gentle as you clean your baby. His skin is sensitive, and these first washings can help prepare him for the next step—the tub filled with water.

Rinsing. Rinse off the soap with a little water, being careful not to get the cord wet. Be especially gentle around your baby's genitals, especially if he's been circumcised. Rinse the washcloth frequently to keep it from spreading germs. Check the folds and crevices in your baby's skin to make sure you got them clean.

Drying. If you want, dry each area after you've washed it, to prevent your baby from getting chilled. Otherwise, dry your baby with a soft towel when you're finished washing. A hooded towel works best because you can keep your baby's head warm. Chat with him as you dry him, using a soft voice and a pleasant look.

96. Splish Splash: Keeping Baby Clean

Some babies love bath time. They giggle, coo, splash, kick, and generally enjoy the water. Other babies don't like it so much. They cry, squirm, and fight the entire process. The best way to achieve bath time bliss is preparation.

Gradual start. Some babies don't enjoy new experiences and need to ease into the tub slowly. Start with a sponge bath so your baby can get used to the feeling of the water, then move to a small bathtub with only a little water so she can get used to the new environment.

Size. A big bathtub may be frightening to a baby who's used to more confined spaces such as an infant seat or crib. Use a smaller tub to begin with, so your baby feels more secure. A smaller tub makes handling your baby easier, too.

Temperature. Make sure the water temperature is comfortable for your baby. Water that's slightly warmer than room temperature is usually okay. Check the temperature occasionally to make sure it's still comfortable.

Security. Babies who don't like the bath may feel insecure in a slippery tub. Hold your unsure baby firmly to keep her from slipping around in the water and to make her feel secure.

Safety. Never ever leave your baby unattended in the bath—not even for a second. She can drown in less than an inch of water.

Prevention. Turn your water heater down to 120°F (49°C) or lower. If the hot-water handle is accidentally bumped, your baby won't be scalded.

Frequency. You don't need to give your baby a bath every day, especially if she doesn't like it yet. Every other day or twice a week is fine in the beginning. Your baby's skin is tender and doesn't need excessive cleaning. Besides, babies don't get very dirty. Just make sure to keep the diaper area clean.

Enjoyment. Bathing your baby is a wonderful way to enhance your bond. Although the primary purpose is cleaning your baby, bath time can soothe a fussy baby, calm a cranky baby, and relax a wakeful baby enough to get her to sleep.

97. Quick Tip: Bath Buffet

Bath time was always a struggle for my older baby. One day I put one of those cafeteria trays in the water and set some plastic food toys on top. He had a ball with the stuff—pouring, serving, pretending to eat what he cooked. Then we "washed" the dishes together and he got out of the bath nice and clean.

—Mia T.

98. Waterworks: Bath Equipment

- Baby bathtub (with a plastic, non-slip surface)
- Bathtub sponge that fits inside the baby tub (for extra support)
- Bathtub ring (if baby gets too big for the small tub)
- Two to four soft washcloths, wash gloves, or washcloth puppets
- Two to three small hooded towels
- Mild baby soap
- Comb or brush
- Bath toys

99. Quick Tip: Cloth Puppet

My baby didn't like bath time, and I couldn't figure out why. I was gentle with her. I was careful to make her feel secure. I tried to make it pleasant—but it just wasn't work-

ing. What finally turned her around was one of those washcloth puppets made for the bath. She loved being washed with it as long as I kept moving it while talking or singing. I bought several more and used different ones each time.

—*Mary W.*

100. Toys in the Tub

Make bath time even more enjoyable with fun, stimulating toys. Being in the water offers a variety of sensations and phenomena for your baby to discover. As he grows and develops, he'll enjoy the water even more.

- Rubber ducks and other squeeze toys
- Animal or puppet washcloths
- Plastic cups, bowls, and spoons
- Turkey basters
- Squirt bottles
- Small plastic pitchers or watering cans
- Plastic and wooden toy boats
- Balls of different sizes
- Plastic bath books
- Strainers and sifters
- Sponges of various shapes and sizes
- Foam toys
- Unbreakable mirrors
- Bathtub activity centers
- Toys that sink and float

101. Rub a Dub Dub: Moving into the Bathtub

When the cord falls off and the circumcision heals, it's time for a regular bath.

Prepare. Set up the equipment ahead of time so you're completely prepared. Make sure the room isn't drafty or cold. (Somewhere between 72°F and 76°F should be fine.) If you're not planning to climb in with your baby, place the plastic baby tub in the regular tub. The baby tub will help control her position and make bathing easier for both of you. If you want, include a body-shaped sponge for extra support.

Add water. Fill the baby tub with a few inches of water for the first bath. Add more as your baby gets used to the sensation. There's no need to fill the bath too full, since this can be dangerous for your baby. Make sure the water temperature is comfortable—not too cool and not too warm.

Introduce baby. Place your baby in the tub and chat with her for a few minutes. Dribble water over her arms and legs to introduce the sensation and demonstrate (hopefully) that the experience is pleasurable. Keep an eye on her at all times.

Wash. Use water and mild soap on your baby's body, but only water on her face. Baby shampoo isn't necessary until your baby has a good head of hair. Until then, mild soap is fine. Don't forget to pay special attention to the folds and crevices of her body.

Play. If your baby is enjoying her bath, let her spend some time playing in the water. Try to have fun with her during bath time. Besides bath toys, supply her with decorative washcloths, safe kitchen gadgets, and other objects that will make the experience pleasurable. Take her in the big tub occasionally and enjoy some bath fun together.

Wrap up. Wrap your baby in a hooded towel and hold her for a few minutes. Praise her and reassure her. Use a soft towel to blot her dry rather than rubbing her tender skin. Take her to the changing table and let her spend a few more minutes naked, if she's warm and enjoying herself. There's no need to use lotions or powders after the bath, especially if your baby has sensitive skin. They can cause more harm than good.

102. Get Me Out of Here!: If Baby Hates the Bath

Here are some tips for helping your baby enjoy his bath.

- Take your time. Rushing the process may make your baby tense.
- Give your baby a massage before, during, or after the bath.
- Make sure the water temperature is comfortable, the bathtub feels secure, and you're holding your baby firmly.
- Give your baby a bath when he's in a good mood.
- Make bath time fun by playing with your baby while he's in the tub.
- Try to make sure the soap doesn't get in your baby's eyes.
- Handle your baby gently as you bathe him.
- Get in the tub with your baby.
- If all else fails, finish up quickly and remove him. Reassure him that he's safe. If he continues to hate tub baths, go back to sponge baths for a while, and gradually make the transition to tub baths when you think he's ready.

103. Quick Tip: Bathing Baby's Baby

When my baby was about eight months old, she started getting bored with her bath. I loaded the tub with plenty of toys, but nothing seemed to work. Finally I brought one of her plastic baby dolls into the water. She started giving it a bath! It was amazing! She imitated what I did. She shampooed her baby's hair, washed her hands and feet, and scrubbed her back. From that point on, she washed her baby while I washed her.

> —Simonie W.

104. Bath Time Play

Here are some fun things you can do with your baby while she's in the tub.

- Read stories and nursery rhymes.
- Sing songs.
- Make funny noises with your hands or mouth.
- Massage her with water.
- Float her on her back (holding her securely).
- Sprinkle her lightly with water.
- Gently splash water around her (being careful not to splash her face).
- Pour water over her arms, legs, and body.
- Put plastic stickers on the side of the tub for her to look at.
- Draw on the side of the tub with special crayons designed for water use.

105. Quick Tip: Dad's Turn

Since I was breastfeeding our baby, I felt like my husband needed his own opportunities for baby care aside from diapering. I decided to turn bath time over to him so he'd have a special experience with our son every day. My husband was very playful with our son in the bath, which they both enjoyed. I think bath time really strengthened their bond.

—Kelly V.

106. Other Bath Time Necessities

Wrap up bath time with cuddling and other activities, as needed.

Brushing hair. Brush your baby's hair to make it look nice and to stimulate the follicles. Brushing helps reduce cradle cap, too.

Trimming nails. Trim your baby's nails after the bath (when they're soft) so she doesn't scratch her face.

Treating diaper rash. Watch for early signs of redness so you can prevent a full-blown rash.

Cleaning the cord stump. Clean the cord stump with cotton balls (or swabs) and alcohol until it dries up and falls off.

Fresh diaper. Give your baby a little naked time before applying a clean diaper.

Fresh clothes. A clean outfit will keep your baby warm and make her look adorable.

Caution: Be extremely cautious with cotton swabs if you plan to clean your baby's ears. Only clean the outer part of the ear (what you can see). Don't put the swab into the ear canal. You can do severe damage to your baby's eardrum if you probe too deeply or lose your grip. Your doctor will examine your baby's ears and ear canals when you go in for checkups.

107. Quick Tip: Baby Shower

My baby hated the bath, but she loved taking a shower with my husband and me. We'd take turns holding her while the other washed up. At first we were careful not to get the spray in her eyes, but soon she was splashing with her hands and didn't mind the spray. I don't know if this works for every baby, but mine loved it. You have to be careful with a soapy baby, though. They're really slippery!
        —Melissa A.

Chapter 6:
Sleeping

108. Nighty Night: Baby's Slumber Style

The need for sleep varies from baby to baby. Most newborns sleep an average of sixteen hours in a twenty-four-hour period. Surprisingly, the average one-year-old sleeps only three hours less than the newborn. These are statistical averages, and your baby may sleep anywhere from nine to eighteen hours a day, all within the range of normal. Here are some important issues to consider.

Activity level. Some babies get sleepy after they've been very active, while others become overstimulated. Watch your baby to see how his activity level affects him, and try to help him deal with it by anticipating his reaction.

Sensitivity to environment. Some babies shut out the noise well, while others are sensitive to every sound. Watch your baby to see how he responds to outside noise, then adjust the environment to suit his needs.

Sleep cycles. Some babies will sleep all night early on, and others will have restless nights for months, depending on their innate sleep cycles. Note your baby's cycle so you can help him change it, if necessary.

Baby's pattern. Allowing your baby to determine his own sleep pattern is usually better than having him conform to yours (unless he's up most of the night, in which case you'll need to reverse his pattern so you can get some sleep).

Evening fussiness. Many babies are fussy in the evening before they settle into a longer sleep. This is normal.

Parents' sleep. If your baby isn't getting enough quality sleep, you're probably not either, which may be causing you to be frustrated, anxious, or impatient. If necessary, alter your baby's sleep pattern by putting him down at the same time each day or night.

Sleep rituals. The best way to help your baby sleep is to establish a routine. Establish a routine that includes rituals such as a taking a bath before bed, hugging a special blanket or lovey, singing lullabies, reading stories, and so on.

Independence. Your ultimate goal is to help your baby learn to go to sleep on his own (and get back to sleep when he wakes up). Put him down when he's tired but not completely asleep. If he wakes up in the middle of the night, wait a few seconds to allow him to soothe himself back to sleep. If his cries become louder, check on him. He may be hungry or upset from a bad dream.

109. Quick Tip: Family Bed

Our baby was an extremely irregular sleeper. We couldn't figure out how to get him into a sleep routine. What finally helped was bringing him into our bed at night. He usually fell asleep lying next to us, and we could get some sleep while he was comforted. Having him in the family bed just made life easier for all of us.

—Chris S.

110. Go to Sleep, My Baby: Inducing Sleep

Experiment with the following ways to get your baby to sleep. Start with the techniques that best fit your style. Give each one several tries before moving on. It may take three or four nights before your baby responds. In the end, your baby should be sleeping better—and so should you.

Quiet play. Help your baby prepare for bedtime by doing quiet activities. Give her a massage or feed her right before bedtime. Don't get her wound up with active play when you want her to settle down.

Create motion. If your baby has trouble getting to sleep, walk her in the front pack, rock her, try the baby swing, or take her for a drive in the car.

Family bed. Let your baby sleep in your bed, if it's comfortable for you. Many parents believe in the family bed philosophy, which is practiced in many cultures. You're not likely to roll over on your baby and hurt her unless you're under the influence of alcohol or drugs. You should realize, however, that the family bed may postpone independent sleep in your baby.

Consistency. Try to be consistent with your baby's bedtime routine so she gets used to a specific pattern.

Security. Swaddle your infant to make her feel secure and to recreate the feeling of being inside the womb.

Reminders. Leave your robe near the crib so your baby can smell you close by.

111. Quick Tip: Baby Bed in the Big Bed

I wanted to let my baby sleep in my bed, but my mother-in-law kept telling me I might roll over on her while asleep. I knew plenty of people who had their babies in bed with them, and that never happened. But I was still worried about it. Then I found this foam bed at a baby store. You place the foam bed in the middle of your big bed, snuggle your baby in, then sleep next to it. The foam border prevents your baby from rolling onto her stomach, and it keeps you from rolling onto your baby. It also makes middle-of-the-night nursing more convenient. I love it!

—Susan W.

112. More Tips on Inducing Sleep

Warmth. Warm the sheets with your hands or a hot-water bottle before putting your baby in bed.

Quiet. Make sure your baby's sleep area is quiet, especially if he's a sensitive sleeper. Turn down the TV or music, lower the telephone ringer, and put a sign on the door asking visitors not to ring the bell or knock loudly.

Soothing sounds. Play calming music or recordings of sounds from the womb, or get a teddy bear that plays lullabies.

White noise. Play recordings of running water, waves lapping on a shore, wind, and so on. Or turn on a fan or other white-noise machine.

Bath. Give your baby a warm, soothing bath to calm him down before bedtime.

Active play. Play actively with your baby well before bedtime, to help him release his pent-up energy. Then cool down with a quiet activity to calm him and get him ready for sleep.

Sleepwear. Put your baby in comfortable sleep clothes (warm, soft, cozy, and loose) to let him know it's sleep time.

Routine checks. Monitor your baby for things that may interfere with his sleep, such as hunger, teething pain, congestion, room temperature, a wet diaper, or some medical problem. Call your doctor if your baby seems ill.

Safety. Make sure your baby is safe during sleep. Remove excess pillows and blankets from his crib. Check to see that he's not overheated. Make sure he's on his back to sleep, and check his clothing to make sure it's not too tight or too loose.

Solid food? Although some babies younger than four months respond to solid food by sleeping through the night, this is usually temporary and may cause more harm than good. Starting solids before four months may result in allergic reactions, upset stomachs, or a full stomach with little room left for the main source of nutrition: milk.

113. Quick Tip: Sleep Serial

Every night I told my baby a story. At first he just listened to the sound of my voice, which seemed to soothe him to sleep. As he got older, he started to enjoy the story. Each night he'd fall asleep in the middle of the latest install-ment, and the next night I'd pick up where I'd left off. We called it "The Never-Ending Story." It's still going on.
—Courtney B.

114. Back to Dreamland: Getting Baby Back to Sleep

Sometimes your baby will wake up for no apparent reason and have difficulty getting back to sleep.

Pat, pat. Pat your baby gently, or lay a soothing hand on her stomach and stroke her.

Sing a song. Sing a lullaby in a soft voice, even if you can't sing.

Wrap up. Swaddle your baby in a cozy blanket so she feels secure.

Play music. Turn on some soft music to calm and relax your baby.

Read a book. The rhythm of your voice may put her back to sleep.

Let her suck. Give your baby a pacifier so she can soothe herself back to sleep. (This can be quite effective, but it may create a dependency.)

Rock on. Rock your baby while standing or sitting in a rocking chair.

Turn on white noise. Turn on a fan, washing machine, vacuum cleaner, or other machine that drowns out other noises.

Find her lovey. Give your baby a special blanket or stuffed animal to help her get back to sleep.

Lend your robe. The smell of your robe in her crib may help her get back to sleep.

Caution: The adage, "Let your baby cry herself to sleep," isn't popular with most child development experts today, at least not in the first six months of life. Your baby cries for a reason. Letting her cry only teaches her that you're not going to be there when she needs you. Babies who are not responded to go through a three-day period of withdrawal, much like the stages of depression, during which they cry for shorter and shorter periods of time. This may cause a break in the emotional connection between parent and baby.

115. Quick Tip: Tummy Filler

One thing that seemed to help my youngest child sleep better (after she turned six months) was giving her a bottle mixed with a little rice cereal right before bed. I blended a couple tablespoons of rice cereal with her formula, and made the hole in the nipple larger so the mixture would flow more easily. It was heartier and more filling, and it seemed to help her sleep longer at night.

—Alison F.

116. Sudden Infant Death Syndrome (SIDS): The Latest on Crib Death

Sudden Infant Death Syndrome (SIDS), also known as crib death, is still not well understood by medical scientists. SIDS occurs when parents put their seemingly healthy babies to bed and find they have died during their sleep for no apparent reason. SIDS is the leading cause of death in the first year of life. It generally occurs between the ages of one month and one year, most commonly between two and six months, and usually between midnight and six in the morning. SIDS occurs more often in males than females, in low-birth-weight babies and premature babies, in babies who show early signs of breathing apnea, in babies with little prenatal care, and in babies of low socioeconomic status.

Here are some of the things you can do to help prevent SIDS.

Back to sleep. Put your baby on his back to sleep. The "Back to Sleep" Campaign has cut the incidence of SIDS in half.

Firm sleep surface. Make sure your baby sleeps on a firm mattress or other firm surface, not on a sheepskin, waterbed, pillow, or other soft surface.

Breastmilk. Breastfeed your baby, if possible.

Fresh air. Don't smoke, and make sure your baby always sleeps in a smoke-free environment.

Early start. Get good prenatal care if you're still pregnant, and take your baby to the doctor for regular checkups after he's born.

Body temperature. Don't overdress your baby or keep the room too warm.

Clear crib. Don't put extra bedding, pillows, or stuffed animals in the crib.

Special equipment. Ask your doctor about a special breathing monitor if there's a predisposition for SIDS in your family.

Preparation. Take an infant CPR class.

117. Noises from Baby's Room: Crying at Slumber Time

Listen carefully to your baby's cries during the night. Fussing, crying, and bloodcurdling screams all require different responses.

Fussy whining. If your baby's just fussing, allow her to continue for a few minutes to give her a chance to go back to sleep on her own.

Full-blown crying. If your baby's cries continue or increase, soothe her so she feels reassured. That may be enough to get her back to sleep. After the first few months, try to avoid feeding your baby during the night, and try to settle her without taking her out of bed.

Frantic screams. If your baby's cries are bloodcurdling screams, attend to her immediately.

118. Quick Tip: Soothing Facial

If your baby is having trouble calming down or getting to sleep, lay him in his crib faceup and lightly stroke his forehead and nose. This should relax his face and eventually his whole body. Hopefully, he'll calm down and fall asleep.
—Taya M.

Chapter 7:
Crying

119. Crying and Fussing: Baby Is Hungry

All babies cry, some more than others. It's their first form of communication, and it's very effective in getting parents to respond. Try to learn your baby's hunger cry so you can quickly determine that he needs food instead of something else.

Feed your baby. If it's not the usual feeding time, try feeding your baby anyway. He may still be hungry.

Be flexible. Let your baby establish an on-demand feeding schedule, rather than putting him on a rigid schedule.

Try a pacifier. Try giving your baby a pacifier between meals, in case he needs more sucking time.

Check weight gain. To make sure your baby is getting enough milk, check to see that he's gaining weight and generally looks healthy. Talk to your doctor if you have any questions.

Change formulas. Some babies have allergies or intolerances to one or more types of formula. Always check with your doctor before trying a different formula.

Offer water. Give your baby a bottle of water between meals to help keep him satisfied.

Call the doctor. If your baby continues to cry and can't be calmed, call your doctor.

120. Quick Tip: Sleep Snack

My baby never seemed satisfied. He'd nurse awhile, then he'd be hungry again an hour later. I tried adding formula, but he only wanted breastmilk. I tried encouraging him to nurse longer so I could get a longer break between feedings, but that didn't work either. At four months I finally started giving him a little rice cereal between meals, even though solid food wasn't recommended until six months. What a difference! That bit of cereal seemed to stick with him longer, so I could feed him every three hours instead of every hour. Guidelines are helpful, but every baby is different.
—Mary W.

121. Crying and Fussing: Baby Is in Pain

When a baby is in pain, the cry is usually sharp and loud. Check for the following causes and talk to your doctor, if necessary.

Diaper rash. Check to see if the diaper area is red and pimply, then apply some diaper rash cream.

Teething. If your baby is drooling, irritable, and putting her fingers or other objects in her mouth, she may be teething. (See page 69.)

Earache. If your baby is rubbing her ear, she may have an ear infection. Check her temperature and call the doctor, if necessary.

Stomachache. If your baby is constipated, gassy, spitty, irritable, or arching her back after a feeding, talk to your doctor about possible interventions.

Diaper pin. Your baby may have a diaper pin pressing against her flesh, so check out her diaper area and fix the pin.

122. Crying and Fussing: Baby Has Colic

Colic is defined as inconsolable crying that occurs for several hours each day, usually in the evening. Colic usually declares itself by two to four weeks, and symptoms usually disappear by four months. It's still poorly understood, but here are some tips for comforting your colicky baby.

- Lay your baby across your knees and gently pat her back.

- Lay your baby on her back and press her legs into a deep knee bend to help expel gas.

- Massage your baby's abdomen in a circular pattern.

- Walk around holding your baby and patting his back.

- Hold your baby in different positions until you find one that's comfortable for her, such as across your arm (football hold) or facing out while you hold her stomach.

- Take your baby for a drive in the car.

- Consider using a device called SleepTight, which replicates the sounds and motion of a car going 50 miles per hour. It costs $100, but many parents have had great success with it. Call 800-NO-COLIC for more information.

123. Quick Tip: Coping with Colic

My baby had colic for the first three months. She'd cry for hours at a time, and nothing seemed to soothe her. I could tell she was in pain, but I didn't know what to do. Some people told me I was tense, which was causing my baby to be tense, but my doctor said that was a myth. He told me my baby probably had GER (gastroesophageal reflux), which is like heartburn. He advised me to keep my baby upright after feeding, avoid foods that seemed to irritate him (I was breastfeeding), offer smaller and more frequent feedings, and wear him as much as possible.
After three months, colic was gone—miraculously. Thank God.

—Bree S.

124. Quick Tip: Walking the Floor

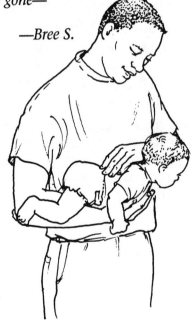

Hold your baby facedown on your arm, then walk around rubbing her back. This should help release her gas and calm her down. Plus, looking at the moving floor may lull her to sleep.
—Tiffany G.

125. Crying and Fussing: Baby Is Distressed

Babies also cry when they're scared, lonely, or bored. After you check for physical problems, try the following tips to calm a distressed baby.

Cuddle up. Hold your baby, talk to him, and keep him close so he feels safe and secure.

Take a walk. Put your baby in a front pack and take a walk to distract him from his distress.

Swing. Put your baby in a baby swing for a few minutes to see if the motion helps calm him down.

Rock. Soothe your baby by nursing him in the rocking chair.

Take a dip. Try giving your baby a warm bath for a change of sensation and environment.

Play. Entertain your baby with funny faces or a special toy.

126. Crying and Fussing: Baby Is Tired

Babies sometimes need help getting to sleep.

Swing. Put your baby in the baby swing, and she'll probably swing herself to sleep.

Walk. Take your baby for a walk in the front pack or stroller to see if the motion puts her to sleep.

Rock. Hold your baby in your arms and sway her, or rock in the rocking chair until she conks out.

Take a drive. Put your baby in the car seat and take her for a drive. When she falls asleep, bring her inside. Never leave her unattended in the car.

127. Quick Tip: Sing a Sleepy Song

I sang each of my children a song every time I put them to sleep. I used different songs for different children, so they each had a special song. A baby learns to associate a particular song with sleep, which helps him relax and drift off. It's a great way to close the day.

—Claire J.

128. Crying and Fussing: Baby Is Sick

Babies cry when they're not feeling well. Common causes include fever, earache, stomachache, or infection. Consider the following symptoms as possible signs of illness, and don't hesitate to call your doctor if you think your baby needs to be seen.

Ear pulling. Your baby is pulling at her ears or rubbing the sides of her face.

Relentless crying. Your baby is crying nonstop and won't be comforted.

Fever. Your baby feels hot to the touch and may have a fever (or you've taken her temperature and confirmed her fever).

Labored breathing. Your baby is having difficulty breathing or is breathing very fast.

Lethargy. Your baby's energy level is way below normal.

Appearance. Your baby is pale or flushed, or she just looks sick.

129. Crying and Fussing: Baby Is Overstimulated

Some babies cry from overstimulation (too much activity or noise) and may have trouble winding down. Here are some tips to help your baby learn to calm himself.

Change the scenery. Move your baby to a quiet room.

Do not disturb. Try to keep your baby on a regular schedule, especially if disruptions upset him.

Don't neglect naps. Give your baby the opportunity to take longer or more frequent naps, but be careful not to let him sleep so much during the day that he isn't tired at night.

Take a break. Remove your baby from an overly stimulating situation, such as a crowd of people, loud noises, or lots of activity.

Soothe your baby. Sing to your baby as you gently sway him back and forth.

130. Crying and Fussing: Baby Is Frustrated—and So Are You

Babies also cry when they get frustrated or angry. Here are some tips for helping your baby (and you) get through a difficult time.

Act fast. Respond to your baby's cries quickly and accurately. Learn his different cries as soon as possible, so you can tend to his needs without wasting time. The sooner you respond, the easier it'll be to calm him down.

Hold tight. Swaddle your baby, hold him close, and talk to him in a soothing voice.

Take a break. Put your baby down for a few minutes in a safe place, and do something soothing such as enjoying a cup of tea, doing relaxation techniques, or calling a friend for support. Then pick up your baby again when you feel refreshed.

Get help. If you find yourself getting tense and irritable, find someone to take care of your baby for a while. (Make sure anyone who looks after your baby is qualified to care for a young child.) Many cities have crisis hotlines for parents to call when they're at risk for hurting their child.

Caution: Never shake your baby in an attempt to calm him down. Shaking a baby can cause brain damage, spinal injuries, and even death. Get help if you're feeling angry and frustrated with your baby.

Chapter 8:
Breastfeeding

131. Breastfeeding Your Baby

Breastmilk is the best nutrition for your baby. It provides nutrients for brain growth, hormones and growth factors not found in formula, and fats that help in tissue growth and nervous system development. Breastmilk protects against allergies, is easier to digest, and is naturally appealing to babies. Research suggests that breastfeeding may reduce the risk of Sudden Infant Death Syndrome (SIDS). Research also suggests that premature babies who receive mother's milk gain higher IQ points over time. Colostrum, the first milk produced by the breasts, contains a high percentage of white blood cells and infection-fighting proteins. It provides babies with natural antibiotics that last for months.

Breastfeeding is great for mothers, too. It enhances your attachment to your baby, helps you burn calories so you lose pregnancy weight more quickly, and releases a hormone that helps return your uterus to its pre-pregnancy size. There's evidence that breastfeeding reduces the incidence of breast cancer in women. Breastmilk saves you money, too, since you don't have to buy formula. Here are some tips to help you get off to a good start with breastfeeding.

Bare it all. Expose your nipples to the air to make them less sensitive.

Towel off. Rub your nipples lightly with a soft towel to toughen them up. Don't be too vigorous, though, or you may stimulate uterine contractions.

Avoid soap. Soap dries your skin, which may cause cracked nipples.

Avoid lotions. Your nipples secrete a natural lubricant.

Twist and shout. Gently pull and twist your nipples if they're flat, to help them protrude more. If your nipples are inverted, check with a lactation consultant for ways to prepare them for nursing.

132. Quick Tip: Choose for Yourself

Try not to listen to other people who tell you how long you should breastfeed. The decision is up to you. I thought I would nurse about two or three months, then switch to a bottle, but I fell in love with breastfeeding. I kept it up for eighteen months and enjoyed every minute of it. I wouldn't trade that time for anything.

—Holly K.

133. Dinner's Ready: When to Feed

On demand. Feed your baby when he's hungry. That's usually every one to three hours in the first few weeks of life. The time between feedings usually lengthens as your baby grows and develops. Try to do a minimum of eight feedings in a twenty-four-hour period.

Good latch. Help your baby latch on to your breast by stroking his cheek with your finger or nipple. This should trigger the rooting reflex, which will help him open his mouth and begin sucking. Wait until your baby's mouth is open wide before inserting your nipple.

Weight gain. It's difficult to know how much milk your baby is getting while breastfeeding, so check his weight from time to time. He'll lose some weight after birth, but he should gain it back after the first week or two. He should double his birth weight by four months and triple it by one year.

Wet diapers. Another way to confirm that your baby's getting enough milk is to check to see that he's producing eight to twelve wet diapers a day and substantial stools at least a few times a day.

Nursing feelings. Some mothers become emotional during breastfeeding and may weep or feel depressed. Try some relaxation techniques to help you stay calm, or talk to your doctor if you're having trouble dealing with your emotions.

134. Aim and Shoot: Breastfeeding Positioning

Breastfeeding provides the perfect opportunity for Mom to take a break from her busy day.

Get comfortable. Choose a chair that provides support and helps you relax. Pad it with extra pillows for added comfort.

Change positions. Try a number of breastfeeding positions if you're not comfortable with your original position. A U-shaped pillow wrapped around your waist may help support your baby and get him in the right position.

Check your baby's airway. Make sure your baby's breathing isn't impeded by your breast or pillows or anything else.

Change breasts. Change sides in the middle of each feeding, and begin each feeding with the breast opposite the one you started with the previous feeding.

Dress comfortably. Wear breastfeeding bras and blouses with hidden compartments that allow you to feed your baby in public without having to show anything. Easy access makes breastfeeding easier for your baby, too.

Enjoy yourself. Keep a book, magazine, or the TV remote handy to help you relax and enjoy the time, especially if your baby nods off.

135. Got Milk?: Producing Nutritious Breastmilk

Basically everything you take into your body goes through your system and into your breastmilk. So avoid things that aren't healthy for you or your baby.

- Don't smoke.
- Eliminate alcohol consumption or reduce your intake to occasional or light drinking. You may want to express and discard your breastmilk after having a drink. Avoid moderate to heavy drinking.
- Cut down on caffeine in coffee and sodas.
- Eat a nutritious diet.
- Drink plenty of fluids.
- Continue taking prenatal vitamins.
- Pay attention to certain foods that may be bothering your baby's digestion, and eliminate them if necessary.
- Always talk to your doctor before taking any medication. Many medications may be taken while breastfeeding.

136. Quick Tip: Thirst Quenching

I found I was always thirsty while breastfeeding. So I kept a cold drink by my side while I fed my baby, and I drank about as much as he did. I later learned that it's a good idea to replace the fluids you lose while breastfeeding, but at the time I was just plain thirsty.

—Holly K.

137. Troubleshooting: Dealing with Breastfeeding Problems

Breastfeeding isn't always easy, especially at the beginning.

Supply and demand. Breastfeeding is based on supply and demand. The more you feed your baby, the more milk you produce. If you need to space the feedings further apart, your milk supply will adjust accordingly.

Letdown. Be ready for your milk to let down in the first twenty-four hours after birth. When it finally comes in, your breasts may become full and firm. Express a little milk to relieve the pressure, or use warm compresses to ease the discomfort. An over-the-counter pain reliever, such as acetaminophen, can also help. Talk to your doctor about safe medications.

Good advice. Get off to a good start by talking to a breastfeeding specialist before leaving the hospital or birth center. If you're having trouble later, don't hesitate to call a lactation consultant or breastfeeding organization.

138. Quick Tip: Warm Milk

When I was first dealing with engorgement, I dampened a cloth diaper and microwaved it for about fifteen seconds, making sure it wasn't too hot. I applied it to my breasts, and my milk flowed easily. It also soothed my breasts and helped my baby latch on better.

—Dana M.

139. Feeding Frenzy: Where to Get Help

If you're having difficulty with breastfeeding, there's lots of support out there.

La Leche League. Contact your local La Leche League group or call 800-LALECHE for more information.

Lactation specialists. Check with your doctor or hospital for referrals to certified breastfeeding experts.

Doctor. Ask your pediatrician, obstetrician, or family practitioner for help.

Hospital. Call the hospital to see if they have visiting nurses who can assist you.

Friends. Talk to friends who've had experience breastfeeding.

Books. There are several excellent books on breastfeeding. Visit your local library or bookstore or ask your doctor for a recommendation.

140. Spew Alert: Spitting Up

Babies spit up frequently in the first few weeks, mainly because their digestive systems are adjusting to a new feeding process. They're used to being fed through their umbilical cords, and now they have to ingest food through their mouths. Babies also spit up when they're jostled, when they drink too much milk, when they swallow air, or when they drink too fast. They usually spit up only a teaspoon or so, so don't be alarmed unless your baby is vomiting very forcefully.

Get a head start. Try to feed your baby before she becomes ravenous, so she doesn't take in too much milk too quickly.

Take a burp break. Burp your baby before starting her on the other breast (or after a few ounces from a bottle) to help her remove the air she's swallowed.

Position your baby. Hold your baby upright after a feeding to help prevent spitting up and to aid digestion.

Hold steady. Don't jostle your baby after a feeding.

Check the nipple. If you're using a bottle, examine the size of the nipple hole and make sure it's not too small or too large.

Weigh in. Weigh your baby once a week to see if she's gaining or losing weight. You can use a baby scale or subtract your weight from your combined weight. Talk to your doctor about any concerns.

Check the color. If your baby's vomit is green, call your doctor.

Give it time. Remember, your baby's digestive system needs time to adjust. Significant spitting up usually diminishes by six months, if not earlier.

141. Quick Tip: Minimize the Milk

My baby did a lot of spitting up in the beginning. I finally talked to a lactation specialist who helped me figure out what to do. My milk virtually poured down my baby's throat at the beginning of each feeding, which caused him to take in too much too quickly. So I starting expressing some milk before having him latch on. Taking a little off the top really did the trick.

—Holly K.

142. Get That Away from Me!: Refusing the Breast

Occasionally your baby may refuse the breast. Here are some possible reasons and tips for fixing the problem.

Obstructed breathing. Make sure your baby's airway isn't impeded by your breast or anything else.

Position. Your baby may not be in a comfortable position. Try readjusting him.

Appetite. Your baby may not be hungry even though it seems like feeding time.

Stomachache. Your baby may be gassy. Try some of the techniques on page 117 for relieving the pain.

Inverted nipples. Your baby may not be able to latch on to your nipple if it's inverted. Pull your nipples out gently and roll them between your fingers to help them protrude, or talk to a lactation consultant about ways to help get your nipples more everted.

Tension. Your baby may be sensing your discomfort. Try to relax, do some deep breathing, and enjoy this special time with your baby.

143. Quick Tip: Nipple Enhancement

My nipples were inverted and didn't protrude no matter what I did. When my baby refused my nipples, my lactation consultant recommended artificial nipples (big, soft, plastic covers that fit over your nipples). They helped draw my nipples out while providing something more substantial for my baby to suck on. It wasn't long before he latched on to my own nipples.

—Melanie E.

144. Quick Tip: Milk Shower

I had trouble with engorged breasts. My mother, who breastfed me, recommended I stand in a warm shower before breastfeeding. The warm water felt great and helped my milk let down. In fact, my milk was spraying all over the shower stall! Releasing some of the milk helped the swelling and took the edge off. So when my baby nursed, it wasn't as painful.

—Karen D.

145. When Sucking Is Painful

Most mothers find nursing a little painful in the beginning, as the nipples adjust to baby's sucking and the uterus contracts to its pre-pregnancy size. The discomfort usually goes away after the first few days. However, if your discomfort lingers, try the following tips for relieving the pain.

Change positions. If your baby's sucking is causing pain, try repositioning her so she sucks in a different way.

See the doctor. If your breast is hot, swollen, red, or painful, you might have a breast infection. Talk your doctor about medication, and continue breastfeeding to help clear the clogged ducts. Your baby already has the germs so you don't need to worry about infecting her.

146. Quick Tip: Pain Relief

I used Lamaze breathing and relaxation tips to help manage the pain during breastfeeding. The visiting nurse recommended taking Tylenol a few minutes before nursing, which also helped. In addition, I applied warm compresses while feeding my baby and cold compresses afterward. It also helped to be distracted, so I watched TV or listened to the radio.

—Simonie W.

147. Ouch!: Sore Nipples

Here are some tips for preventing and helping sore nipples.

Get your baby latched on properly. Make sure your baby is taking in the whole nipple, not just the tip, and make sure her lips are pressed out, not in. Wait until your baby's mouth is wide open before inserting your nipple.

Air dry. Air out your nipples frequently to promote and maintain healthy skin.

Change sides. If you develop a cracked nipple, let your baby nurse from the other side so the sore one can heal.

Lubricate. Use lanolin (Lansinoh®) on your nipples to ease the soreness.

Cover up. If your nipples are really sore, cover them with a protective rubber nipple during nursing, but only if advised by a lactation specialist.

148. Quick Tip: Sore from Sucking

My home nurse recommended tea (of all things) for my sore nipples. She made a pot, poured me a cup, then put the teabags on my nipples for a few minutes. The teabags soothed my nipples, and the tea calmed my nerves.

—Holly K.

149. Mega Melons: Swollen, Engorged Breasts

When your milk first comes in, your breasts may become swollen, hard, and painful. This can also happen if you skip a feeding or produce too much milk. Here are some tips to ease the pain of swollen breasts.

Feed your baby. It's the most efficient way to get the milk out of your breasts, and it's good for your baby, too!

Use warm compresses. A warm washcloth may help ease the pain and release your milk.

Take a shower. A warm shower or bath may help your milk let down.

Express some milk. Use your hands or a breast pump to express excess milk from your breasts.

Use a good bra. Make sure your breasts are adequately supported by a good breastfeeding bra.

Use breast pads. Breast pads absorb the milk that leaks from your breasts. Change them frequently to prevent infection.

150. The Little Nipper: Biting

Here are some tips for dealing with your baby's biting during nursing.

Just say no! If your baby bites you during breastfeeding, pull back quickly and tell him, "No!" or, "Ouch!" to let him know that biting hurts you. Then give him another chance to nurse.

NO! NO! If he bites you again, remove your breast and tell him, "No!"

Stop the feeding. If he continues to bite, put your breasts away for a while and do something else with him.

Don't take it personally. Your baby is experimenting with his mouth, and he's probably fascinated by your reaction. He'll eventually learn that biting stops the flow of food, and he won't want that to happen.

151. Quick Tip: Aggressive Eater

My baby was really vigorous at the beginning of a feeding. When one of my nipples began to crack, I started him on the healthy side first. By the time I switched to the tender side, he had lightened up a lot. I also used nipple cream on the cracked nipple, which helped it get better.

—Chris S.

152. Nodding Off: Baby Falls Asleep

Sometimes your baby falls asleep while nursing. This is fine if it comes at the end of a feeding, but if your baby is routinely falling asleep at the beginning of feedings, she may not be getting enough milk. Here are some tips for helping her nurse more.

Wake her up. If your baby is a newborn, wake her for feeding if she sleeps longer than four to five hours at one time. In the first weeks, make sure she gets a minimum of eight feedings in a twenty-four-hour period. If your baby is older, you can let her sleep longer and try feeding her when she wakes up.

Play with her. Play with your baby before the feeding to encourage her appetite.

Pick alert times. Feed your baby near the end of her wakeful period, while she's still alert.

Change sides. If your baby starts to nod off during a feeding, try switching her to your other breast to wake her up.

Relax. Don't worry about the occasional mid-nursing nap if your baby is gaining weight and looking healthy.

153. Quick Tip: Nursing Twins

I joined the Mother of Twins Club after I had my twins. The people there were very helpful with my breastfeeding concerns. I didn't know whether to feed my twins at the same time or take turns with them. The staff recommended I feed them at the same time; otherwise, I might spend my entire day nursing. Plus, I'd be less likely to get confused and feed the same baby twice!

—Chris S.

154. Quitting Time: When and How to Wean

Sometimes babies decide it's time to stop, and sometimes mothers decide it's time to quit nursing. Many factors may be involved in your decision to stop breastfeeding.

End on your own terms. Decide for yourself how long you want to breastfeed. If you're planning to return to work outside the home, consider acquiring a breast pump if you want to continue providing breastmilk to your baby.

Ignore unsolicited advice. People usually mean well, but try to ignore friends and others who encourage you to wean earlier or later than you want. Do what feels right for you and your baby.

Be flexible. Don't pressure yourself to make a decision ahead of time about how long to breastfeed. You can always see how it goes, then quit when unforeseen circumstances arise or you or your baby decides it's time.

Consider doctors' advice. The American Academy of Pediatrics recommends breastfeeding for at least one year. By then babies have outgrown most food allergies and can handle solid foods more easily.

Anticipate the possibility of depression. Hormone levels change during weaning, so you may experience some emotional ups and downs. This is normal but not always easy to deal with. Talk to your doctor if you're having trouble managing your emotions.

Wean gradually. When you begin weaning, ease off one feeding at a time over a period of weeks. Don't try to quit cold turkey. It'll be hard on both of you.

Enjoy the last moments. Many babies have a hard time letting go of nighttime feedings, and you may, too. Extend them as long as you like.

Consider weaning directly to a cup. If your baby is able to handle a sippy cup, you may want to wean directly to that instead of a bottle.

Just add food. As your baby's intake of solid food increases, he may cut down on breastfeeding on his own. Talk to your doctor about this transition.

Prepare for some regression. Your baby may want to nurse at times during the weaning process, which is normal and usually temporary.

155. Quick Tip: Weaning Worries

I had trouble weaning my third baby. My lactation consultant advised me to eliminate the least favorite feeding first. I substituted a bottle for one feeding, then two, then three, and so on. I always sat in different places when bottle-feeding, so my baby wasn't reminded of breastfeeding. I also had my husband do some bottle-feedings. Eventually it worked.

—Simonie W.

Chapter 9:
Formula-Feeding

156. Formula-Feeding Your Baby

Some women are not able (or choose not) to breastfeed. Mothers who feel guilty about not breastfeeding deserve reassurance that they're doing what's best for themselves and their babies. A mother who's anxious or unhappy about breastfeeding isn't doing what's best for her family.

There are some obvious advantages to formula-feeding. Partners can more easily participate in feeding the baby, and babysitters can feed the baby while parents enjoy time to themselves. Formula-feeding frees mothers from worrying about modesty, and allows them to return to work more easily. Formula-feeding may also make you feel less tied down to your baby.

On the other hand, formula-feeding is more expensive than breastfeeding. It also involves more work in the form of mixing, testing temperature, cleaning bottles, and so on. A particular formula may not agree with your baby, and it may take some time to find one that works. Perhaps most importantly, formula does not contain the digestive enzymes or disease-fighting immune factors found in breastmilk. If you decide (or circumstances require you) to formula-feed your baby, there are some important issues to consider.

Check with your doctor. Before you decide what kind of formula to buy, talk to your doctor. Discuss the choices and ask your doctor which formula would be best.

Choose a preparation. Decide which preparation works best for you:

- Powdered (Add water, mix well, and serve.)
- Liquid concentrate (Add water, stir, and serve.)
- Ready-to-feed

Check the date. When buying formula, be sure to check the expiration date. Don't buy formula in damaged cans because it may be tainted.

Make sure it's iron-fortified. The American Academy of Pediatrics recommends formula that is iron-fortified, so make sure to check the label.

Consider milk-based. Most formulas are cow's-milk-based. In other words, they contain animal protein as the source of nutrition.

Consider soy-based. Soy-based formula is less allergenic to some babies than cow's milk. However, some babies are allergic to both, and soy formula may lead to soy allergies later in life.

Consider other formulas. Check with your doctor about special situations in which you would need to use other formulas.

157. Quick Tip: No Bottle Blues Here

I tried to breastfeed my baby, but it just didn't work out for me. So I switched to the bottle. I felt guilty at first, thinking I'd let my baby down in some way, but I actually loved formula-feeding. I always held my baby close when I fed him. It was a special time. I enjoyed the fact that my husband or babysitter could feed the baby, and I didn't have to worry about what I ate or drank or the clothing I wore. I wish breastfeeding had worked, but I was very happy with formula-feeding. I just wish other people hadn't been so critical of me. That was the only disadvantage.

—Carly C.

158. Bottle-Feeding Gear: Bottles and Nipples

You'll need six to ten bottles and nipples on hand when you begin bottle-feeding your baby. Angled bottles that contain plastic bags usually work best, since the milk is more accessible and your baby doesn't take in excess air. You may need to experiment with different combinations of bottles and nipples before finding the one that works best for your baby. Here are some tips on what to look for.

Types of Bottles
- Traditional plastic ones that come in different shapes and sizes
- Ones with disposable liners that squeeze out excess air
- Ones with colorful decorations to stimulate your baby
- Ones that come with different nipples
- Ones that can be sterilized in the dishwasher

Types of Nipples
- Expandable nubbin (round, flat, stubby, more like a mother's nipple)
- Standard bulb (most common, easy to use)
- Orthodontic (relatively new, shaped to fit the mouth)
- Silicone (odor-free and taste-free)

159. Formula-Feeding: How Much?

Formula is digested more slowly than breastmilk, so the time between feedings is usually longer. Individual babies differ, but here are the general guidelines for formula-feeding at various ages.

Birth to one month: ½–2 ounces per feeding for the first day, quickly increasing to 2–3 ounces.

One to three months: 3–4 ounces per feeding.

Three to six months: 4–7 ounces per feeding, or 32 ounces per day.

Six to nine months: 6–8 ounces per feeding, or 20–25 ounces per day as solid foods get established.

160. Formula-Feeding: What Time?

Here are three options to consider.

On demand. Feed your baby when she shows signs of hunger.

On a schedule. Feed your baby every two to three hours in the first few months, and every three to four hours later on (at a relatively fixed time).

Combination. Aim for a general schedule, but feed your baby when she's hungry. This method seems to work best for most babies and parents.

Caution: Don't use a bottle as a pacifier, or your baby may gain too much weight. If your baby seems hungry all the time, extend the time between feedings by playing with your baby, using a pacifier to satisfy her sucking need, or serving a bottle of water occasionally.

161. Formula-Feeding: Getting Started

Heat it. Heat the bottle by running it under hot water or dipping it in a pan of hot water. Avoid microwaving, since it poses the risk of uneven heating and subsequent scalding.

Mix it. Stir or shake the bottle to make sure the formula is evenly distributed.

Test it. Spray a little on your hand or arm to make sure it's not too warm.

Size it. Check the nipple hole. If it's too big, your baby could choke as too much formula pours down his throat. If it's too small, he may not get enough milk.

Enjoy it. If your baby is taking the milk well and thriving, you're doing what's best for everyone.

Keep him steady. Don't jiggle your baby after feeding, or he may spit up.

Toss the leftovers. Don't store unfinished formula in the bottle. It may develop bacteria.

Stay with it. Stick with the same formula unless your baby is having trouble. Check with your doctor before switching.

Sterilize. Clean the bottles and nipples in soapy water or the dishwasher.

162. Formu-Love: Formula-Feeding and Bonding

Parents who formula-feed their babies can bond with them just as closely as breastfeeding parents bond with their babies.

Hold your baby. Always hold your baby when you formula-feed him.

Touch your baby. Stroke, caress, and massage your baby while feeding him. The soothing physical contact will greatly enhance attachment.

Caution: Never prop a bottle while feeding your baby. This will not only impair his attachment and overall development, he may choke on the milk as it pours down his throat.

163. Quick Tip: Cold Milk

I was told to heat the bottles of formula before giving them to my baby, but one night she was so hungry and upset, I just gave her a bottle right out of the refrigerator. She wolfed it down! I stopped heating bottles from that point on, and she never seemed to mind. She was always in a hurry to get her bottle when she was hungry.

—Mary W.

164. Burping and Spitting Up: Helping Baby's Digestion

Some babies burp easily while others hardly ever burp. The trick is getting your baby to burp without causing her to spit up.

Stand up. Hold your baby upright, facing you, with her head at your shoulder. Pat her gently on the back.

Sit up. Place your baby in a sitting position, lean her forward, and pat her gently on the back.

Lay down. Place your baby facedown on your lap, and pat her gently on the back.

Take burp breaks. Burp your baby halfway through a feeding instead of waiting until the end.

Try again. If you're not successful at first, try burping her a few minutes later. It may take a couple of tries.

Accept it. If your baby doesn't burp but seems comfortable, let it go. She may not need to burp.

165. Quick Tip: Out, Out, Baby Spot!

Always have a good supply of stain remover on hand to get out those pesky spit-up and blow-out stains. And always wear a diaper or small towel on your shoulder to protect your clothes.

—Cindy J.

166. Feeding Problems

Some babies have problems digesting a particular type of formula. Watch for the following signs of trouble, and check with your doctor before changing formulas.

- Crying after feeding
- Vomiting after feeding
- Diarrhea
- Constipation
- Gassiness
- Fussiness
- Inconsolable crying
- Irritability after feeding
- Rash

Caution: Giving your baby juice from a bottle can do more harm than good. Most juices provide only a few nutrients, and drinking too much juice may prevent the adequate intake of healthier foods. If your baby falls asleep with a bottle of juice in his mouth, the high sugar content may cause tooth decay and gum problems. Don't put your baby down to sleep with a bottle of juice (or milk), and water down his juice bottles to dilute the sugar. Better yet, use water as a substitute for milk and avoid the juice problem completely.

167. From Bottles to Cups: Weaning

Many pediatricians suggest weaning a baby from a bottle by the end of the first year, primarily because continued bottle-feeding will threaten the health of your baby's teeth.

Use a sippy cup. Provide your baby with a covered sippy that won't spill when tipped over. It provides an effective transition from a bottle to a regular cup.

Skip a meal. Eliminate your baby's least favorite meal first (usually mid-morning or afternoon), and maintain the bedtime feeding until the end of the weaning period.

Avoid reminders. Don't feed your baby in the usual places, so you can avoid triggering an unwanted response.

Limit bottles. Don't let your baby have a bottle other than at mealtime. That way he won't suck on it all day.

Have fun. Provide your baby with lots of fun plastic cups, and talk about how big kids use cups.

"Forget" the bottle. If you go on a trip, accidentally "forget" to bring the bottle. If you "lose" it when you get home, your baby may forget about it, too.

Pacify your baby. Provide pacifiers or other chewy toys during the transition period.

Chapter 10:
Starting Solid Foods

168. Yummy in the Tummy: Starting Solid Foods

Good nutrition is essential for your baby's overall growth and development. Your baby's primary source of nutrition during the first year is breastmilk or formula. We now know that solids should be delayed until at least four to six months, when your baby's digestive tract is better prepared to handle solid food and when the risk of having an allergic reaction is reduced. Other signs that your baby may be ready include the following: her birth weight has doubled, she has good head and neck control, she can sit up with support, she can show you she's full, and she's interested in what you're eating. Here are some tips for introducing solids to your baby.

Birth to six months. Give your baby primarily breastmilk or formula for the first four to six months. Babies' appetites vary, but around six months some babies seem to want more than just milk. Watch your baby for signs of readiness, such as showing intense interest in what you eat.

Six months. Your baby's first meal should be plain rice cereal. It's easily digested, iron-fortified, and not likely to cause an allergic reaction. Mix it with breastmilk or formula until it looks like thin gravy.

Seven to nine months. Next you can offer your baby either a fruit such as bananas, pears, or applesauce, or a vegetable such as squash or peas. Some babies have a definite preference for sweets, while others don't seem to care. Some parents give their babies vegetables first because they're worried they won't eat them after they've tasted fruits. Introduce one food at a time, and wait several days before introducing the next, to make sure your baby isn't allergic.

Nine to twelve months. After your baby's had a variety of fruits and vegetables and is handling them well, you can try meats, such as lamb, veal, or poultry, if you like. Don't serve your baby egg whites, wheat, and cow's milk until the end of the first year. Your baby should be ready for finger foods, too.

Caution: Your baby's stools are likely to change color after solids are introduced. However, if your baby develops diarrhea, vomiting, wheezing, or a skin rash, she may be having an allergic reaction. Stop the food and call your doctor.

169. Quick Tip: Make Your Own

I never used commercial baby foods. I started my baby on home cooking right from the start, around seven months. I bought a small, inexpensive food grinder and set it on the table with our dinner. I put my son in his highchair and ground up the fruits and vegetables we were eating. It was incredibly easy, convenient, and inexpensive.

—Beth M.

170. Focus on Food: Snack Facts

Here are some more tips for feeding your baby.

Take your time. Give your baby several days to get used to each new food before trying another one. That way you'll know the food won't cause digestive or allergy problems.

Watch tongue thrust. Your baby has a tongue thrust reflex that causes him to push food out of his mouth. This reflex usually disappears around four months. It may take him some time to learn how to keep food in his mouth and swallow it.

Monitor reactions. Watch for signs of an allergic reaction, such as skin rash, diarrhea, vomiting, and wheezing.

Don't overfeed. Stop feeding your baby if he starts turning his head, pursing his lips, thrusting his tongue continuously, or fussing. He's probably had enough.

Encourage self-feeding. Encourage self-feeding so your baby can learn to manage food and utensils by himself, further developing his skills and independence. Your baby may be able to handle finger foods around seven or eight months.

Limit sugary juices. Don't serve your baby too many sweet juices, such as apple juice, unless you water them down first. Avoid citrus juices, which are too acidic for your baby. Most juices contain only sugar and vitamin C. If your baby drinks too much juice, he may end up consuming fewer healthy foods necessary for proper growth.

Avoid additives. Don't add salt, sugar, or other additives to your baby's food.

Make it fun. Don't shovel food into your baby's mouth. He may choke or gag. Instead, entice him with games such as Airplane or Choo Choo. Be patient and gentle when feeding your baby, so he enjoys the experience.

171. Quick Tips: Smooth Servings

My baby only liked foods that had a smooth texture. That made sense, I guess, since he was used to milk. I avoided lumps by making sure his food was well mashed or blended. After a while, I started introducing little chunks of food, but he kept spitting them out. I kept trying, though, and he eventually got used to them.

—Julie B.

172. Diet Delays:
Foods to Watch Out For

The following foods may cause allergic reactions in children. Delay them as noted (or at least until the end of the first year).

- Cow's milk
- Egg whites (yolks okay after nine months)
- Peanuts (after four years)
- Wheat products (except baby cereal)
- Honey
- Corn
- Fish and shellfish

Caution: Help prevent eating disorders later in life by making feeding time enjoyable for your baby. Talk cheerfully, play games, and don't punish your baby for not eating. If she'd rather play with her food than eat it, let her. Playing with food is an important learning experience. However, if she starts throwing her food, stop the feeding (or remove her from the highchair) and explain in clear and simple terms that food is not to be thrown.

173. Super Food: Good Nutrition for Your Baby

You should introduce your baby to a wide variety of healthy foods when she's ready for solids. Here are some important elements of a healthy diet:

- Vitamin A (apricots, cantaloupe, carrots, spinach, sweet potatoes)
- Vitamin C (oranges, grapefruit, tomatoes)
- High-fiber (apples, bananas, plums, pears, strawberries, peas, potatoes, spinach)
- Vegetables (broccoli, cauliflower, Brussel sprouts, cabbage)

Avoid processed foods, highly sweetened or salty foods, or food additives. Also, don't put your baby on a diet if you're concerned about her weight. Talk to your doctor for advice on a healthy nutrition program.

Bonus tip: Instead of encouraging your baby to eat large meals, allow her to snack throughout the day. She can sit and join you at regular mealtimes, but don't expect her to eat a lot at one sitting.

174. Down the Hatch: Feeding Tips

Here are some tips to help get your baby to eat.

Utensils. Let your baby use baby spoons and forks to learn how to handle food and to help him get used to feeding himself.

Small bites. Cut the food into small pieces, if necessary, so your baby can manage the mouthfuls.

Proper amount. Don't overload your baby's plate with food. It may seem overwhelming to him.

Don't push. Don't make your baby clean his plate, and don't force him to have seconds. This can lead to obesity. Let him stop eating when he feels full.

Big tray. Get a highchair with a big tray to contain the inevitable mess. Then let your baby enjoy his food.

Plastic bib. Buy a plastic bib with a pocket at the bottom for catching food that drops from your baby's mouth or utensils. It reduces the amount of food that winds up on the floor and your baby's clothes, and cleanup is a breeze. You simply rinse out the bib and set it on the drying rack for next time.

Feeding fun. Make feeding time fun by playing games, singing songs, and so on.

175. Quick Tip: Try, Try Again

My baby was a very picky eater. He didn't like any food the first time around. Eventually I learned that if I tried again a week or two later, he liked it. Apparently it took a while for him to get used to the taste. This didn't work all the time, but hey, I didn't like broccoli until I was almost thirty.

—Mia T.

176. Quick Tip: Fun Foods

When my third child started eating solids, I tried to make it fun for him because my other babies had been really finicky. I lined up his peas in creative rows, put his baby food in fun bowls, used cartoon spoons, and served his milk in colorful cups. Later on I made funny-face pancakes, cookie-cutter sandwiches, wagon-wheel macaroni, and fruit yogurt parfaits. Making his food entertaining was fun for him—and for me, too.

—Barbara S.

177. Me Do It!: Self-Feeding

Here are some tips for helping your baby learn to feed herself.

Six to nine months

- Put your baby in her highchair and set bits of food on the tray.
- Feed her with a baby spoon and let her play with the spoon while she eats.
- Offer her a sippy cup to practice with.

Nine to twelve months

- Offer your baby lumpier foods, if she's handling her food well.
- Include her in the family meal by placing her in her highchair near the table, even if she's not particularly hungry.

Caution: Always supervise your baby while she's eating, in case she chokes on a bite of food. Be careful that she doesn't stuff too much food in her mouth.

178. Fun Finger Foods

Finger foods are fun to eat, and they help develop your baby's fine motor skills. Here are a few options.

- Dry, unsweetened cereal
- Frozen or cooked peas
- Soft, cooked chunks of carrots, zucchini, and squash
- Small chunks of soft cheese
- Small, cooked chunks of potatoes and sweet potatoes
- Teething biscuits
- Small chunks of avocado
- Small pieces of cooked, nonwheat pasta (rice pasta)
- Soft tofu cubes
- Banana bites
- Small chunks of soft fruit (canned pears, cooked apples)

179. Quick Tip: Let Baby Do It

I think babies are much more capable than parents realize. They figure out lots of things on their own, such as how to hold a spoon and feed themselves. I tried not to do too much for my baby. Instead, I showed him how something was done, and I encouraged him to figure it out for himself. It was time consuming in the beginning, but in the long run I taught him to be more self-sufficient.

—Susan W.

180. Quick Tip: Bottle Cup

I helped wean my baby to a cup in a fun way that I've shared with other parents, who said it worked really well. First I removed the nipples from formula bottles, and inserted straws. My baby loved holding his familiar cartoon bottle and sucking from the straw. Eventually we moved to a regular cup with a straw. And finally he drank straight from a cup.

—Esther S.

Chapter 11:
Baby's Clothing, Gadgets, and Equipment

181. Room with a Coo: Baby's Environment

Here are some tips for decorating your baby's room.

Baby themes. There are lots of options to give your baby's room a sense of color, creativity, and fun. Consider one of the following popular baby themes: teddy bears, animals, trains, circus items, toys, balls, balloons, Mother Goose (or other nursery rhyme) characters, picture book characters, or cartoon characters.

Neutral environment. You might prefer a less specific environment early on, one that will grow with your child over time. For example, you might choose a neutral color and decorations that can be easily exchanged.

Wallpaper versus paint. Decide whether you prefer wallpaper, which may have to be torn off and replaced over time, or paint, which may have to be repainted over the years. Both require some upkeep, but each can be changed as your baby grows and develops new interests.

Bright colors. Infants are attracted to bright, bold primary colors such as red, blue, and yellow, so you might want to paint or wallpaper in those colors, or use them as accessories in the room.

Alternatives. Instead of choosing wallpaper or bright colored paint, you may prefer large colorful decals, baby-related posters or wall hangings, fabrics, three-dimensional objects (such as toys), or lots of mirrors.

182. Pitter Patter of Little Feet: Flooring

Your baby will spend quite a bit of time on the floor, so here are some tips for floor coverings.

Carpet. Carpeting is nice and soft for your baby as she begins to crawl. It's cozy for you, too, during those late-night or early morning feedings. Invest in stain-guard carpeting, since it repels spills and other messes, and consider a color or pattern that will hide the stains you don't get to in time.

Bare floors. Hardwood floors can be fun for your baby as she learns to crawl and walk. They may provide better grip, too, for bare hands and feet. You might add throw rugs here and there, but make sure they grip the floor so your baby doesn't slip and fall. The downside is hardwood floors can be tough on your baby's head as she leans forward and occasionally falls facedown on the floor.

Combination. Having both carpeting and hardwood floors in your home is ideal for your baby, so she gets the opportunity to develop her gross motor skills on both surfaces.

Bonus tip: An easy-to-clean surface is preferable in your baby's room, since you're bound to have messes to clean up. A small, handheld carpet shampooer may take care of small stains quickly. Make sure you can easily spot small objects that your baby may find and put in her mouth.

183. See the Light: Lighting and Layout

Overhead light. It's nice to have an overhead light in your baby's room, so he can see well when he wants to play. Make sure it isn't too bright and doesn't shine directly in his eyes.

Side lamps. Side lamps may be better because the light is indirect. Make sure you use the right wattage and a safe shade to keep lamps from becoming fire hazards. Secure floor lamps to the wall and keep electrical cords out of your baby's way.

Night-light. A night-light is handy when you need to feed or comfort your baby in the middle of the night. Some babies sleep better when there's a light on.

Arrangement. You'll probably spend lots of time rearranging the items in your baby's room as he gets older and better able to move around. Plan extra space for new equipment (toys, books, stuffed animals) that will be coming in during the first year.

Accessibility. Keep the changing table easily accessible and near the crib, if possible. If you have to leave your baby for a few seconds, you can put him safely in his crib.

Safety. Avoid putting your baby's bed by a window, strong light, or draperies with cords. Secure all furniture that can be climbed and tipped over. Make sure outlets are covered with childproof caps.

184. Room for More: Extras

Play area. Create a cleared area for your growing baby so he can play with his toys, blocks, art supplies, books, and so on. You may want to include a beanbag chair for his comfort while he's doing quiet activities.

Table and chair set. As your baby gets older, add a table and chair set so he has a place to sit and work or play.

Aesthetics. Enhance your baby's room with posters of babies, cartoon characters, book covers, or brightly colored graphics. Hang up mobiles to attract your baby's attention, and put a mirror in the room so your baby can see himself.

Rocking Chair. If you have an extra rocking chair, put it in your baby's room for late-night nursings and comfort calls.

Growth chart. Set aside an area to showcase your baby's growth and development. Hang a measuring tape to mark your baby's height, and have a place to show off your baby's artwork, photos, and mementos.

Bonus tip: Make sure the room is comfortable (somewhere between 70°F and 74°F). Don't heat the room too warmly, and check to see that there are no drafts, leaks, mold, or paint chips in the room.

185. Cute Couture: Dressing Your Baby

One of the joys of parenthood is dressing your baby in cute little outfits and colorful play clothes. The problem is, babies outgrow their clothes very quickly. What's a parent to do?

Exchange duplicate gifts. Go through the gifts you received at your baby showers, and see if you have several similar (or duplicate) items that can be exchanged for things you still need or larger sizes to be used later.

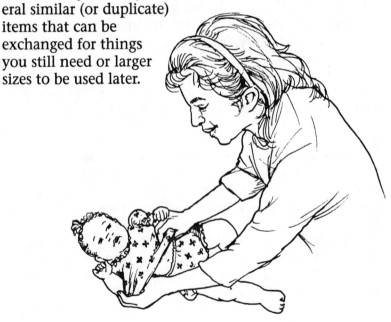

Friends and family. Talk to your friends and family members about borrowing baby clothes that aren't being used. If the other parents are finished having kids, they may let you keep the clothes. Most parents are happy to get rid of baby gear that won't be used again, to make room for all the other stuff that's constantly flowing in.

Catalogs. Consider using catalogs for ease of shopping and good values. Check parenting magazines and the Internet for catalog resources.

Garage sales. They can be a great resource for good clothes at bargain prices. Babies usually wear their clothes for a short time, so you're likely to find them in good shape.

Sales. Watch for sales at local discount or department stores, especially on past-season clothes.

Homemade. If you like to sew, consider making your own baby clothes. Most of your baby's early outfits are easy to make, if you have the time and energy.

Secondhand stores. You can find quality clothing and baby gear at excellent prices. Storeowners have already screened the items for defects and wear, so you're even more likely to find good stuff.

Caution: Be sure to wash all new or secondhand clothes thoroughly before putting them on your baby. New clothes may have chemicals on them and second-hand clothes may still have dirt or germs.

186. More on Dressing Your Baby

Safety. Make sure your baby's sleepwear is flame resistant or snug-fitting (or both). Check for loose buttons, ribbons, or other small or potentially harmful items your baby could choke on.

Access. Buy baby clothes that are easy to put on and take off. Dealing with lots of buttons and snaps may become frustrating for both you and your baby.

Fabric. The best fabric for your baby is cotton, since it breathes and is soft and comfortable. Polyester and other synthetic fibers can be warm, scratchy, uncomfortable, and may cause an allergic reaction.

Gender differences. Boys and girls wear similar outfits in the first year or two (onesies, rompers, T-shirts, and so on). Some parents like to dress girls in frilly dresses and boys in little suits, but boys don't mind wearing pink and girls don't mind wearing blue.

Larger sizes. Buy baby clothes in slightly larger sizes so your baby can wear them a bit longer. Make sure the clothes aren't so big that they tangle him up and limit his movements.

Temperature. Don't overdress your baby in warm weather, thinking he needs to be warm no matter what the temperature is. Put a hat on him in cool weather, since he loses heat quickly through his exposed head.

187. Designer-Baby Basics: What Your Baby Needs

There are some basic outfits your baby will need in the first year to keep him warm, comfortable, and cute. You don't need to overbuy. See how often you use each item, then get more if you find a particular outfit or article of clothing that works well for your baby. If your baby outgrows an outfit he's worn only once or twice, you can probably resell it at a consignment shop or garage sale. Here are some tips for what to have on hand.

- 3–4 dozen diapers
- 2–4 plastic pants (for cloth diapers)
- 2–4 sleepers for bed or naptime
- 4–6 pairs of socks or booties
- 6–8 undershirts or "onesies"
- 3–5 rompers
- 2 hats, one for sun protection and one for warmth
- 1 sweater
- 1 bunting with hood
- 6–8 receiving blankets
- 3–4 diaper covers or waterproof pants (if you're using cloth diapers)

188. Everything but the Kitchen Sink: Baby's Bag

Leaving home with your baby may feel like a major project when you consider all the things your baby may need while you're away. Avoid problems by getting a good diaper bag and packing wisely. There are lots of options out there, so here are some tips to help you find the bag that's right for you.

Match your style. With all the colorful, decorative, and fun diaper bags on the market, choose one that fits your style. Remember, you'll be taking it with you every time you go out, so make sure it's something you can live with.

Lots of pockets. Choose a bag with lots of compartments for bottles, diapers, pacifiers, snacks, toys, and other items. That way it'll be easy to find everything.

Shoulder strap. You'll probably want a bag with a strap that can be slung over your shoulder, so you can keep your hands free for your baby.

Lightweight. You'll be filling it with baby stuff and lugging it around town, so make sure it's lightweight to begin with.

Tough. Get a sturdy bag that's built to last. You don't want a cheap one that's likely to tear or fall part easily, spilling all your gear on the sidewalk or floor.

Travel tote. Consider buying a travel bag with wheels if you have a lot of stuff and prefer to roll it behind you rather than carry it.

Backpack. If you like to carry your baby in a front pack, you might prefer stowing your gear in a backpack.

Super purse. If you want something more discreet and fashionable (so it doesn't look like a baby bag), buy an oversized purse.

Beach bag. During warmer months, try a beach bag that's lightweight, fun, airy, and designed for the surf and sand.

Minibag. For quick trips that require only a diaper, wipes, and maybe a snack, use a minibag (small diaper bag designed for short trips).

189. Diaper Bag Baggage: What You Absolutely Need

It's better to take too much than to forget something, but try not to overload your diaper bag. After all, you'll be the one carrying all that weight. Here's a list of things you may need.

- Several diapers
- Premoistened disposable baby wipes
- Diaper rash cream
- Portable, washable changing pad
- Plastic bags for storing wet diapers until they can be disposed of
- Extra outfit or two
- Pacifiers
- Toys, teethers, and stuffed animals
- Bottles of formula and water
- Burp towel
- Snacks (if your baby is eating solid food)
- Bib
- Blanket
- Socks, hat, mittens, and sweater (for colder weather)
- Baby sun block, sun hat, and sunglasses (for warmer weather)
- First-aid supplies and emergency medical information (See page 187.)

190. Sizing Up Shoes: Walk Wear

To help your baby get off on the right foot, here are some tips for choosing the right shoes for your baby.

Wait a while. Your baby doesn't need walking shoes during the first year of life. He's not likely to start walking until the end of his first year (or later).

Have him go barefoot. Allowing your baby to go barefoot offers him the opportunity to explore his toes and feet, push off the floor, and generally get around more easily. Shoes are mostly decorative in the first year. They can be cumbersome and slippery and interfere with crawling and pre-walking skills, so put them on your baby only when necessary. When your baby starts walking, it's best to have him in bare feet, as long as the surface is safe.

Good fit. When it's time to buy shoes, have a children's shoe clerk help you with the first pair so you get a good fit. Make sure the shoe has plenty of toe room, is flexible, is not too constricting, and doesn't rub. Soft-soled shoes are best.

Save money. There's no need to spend a lot of money on baby shoes in the first year. Babies outgrow them almost as quickly as their clothing (about every three to four months). In fact, your baby's foot will grow to five times its original size by the time he's an adult.

191. Driver Education: Taking Baby on Long Trips

When you're planning a longer trip with your baby, you may want to pack a second bag containing extra essentials and other items that will help pass the time, prevent boredom, and make traveling fun. Here are some items to consider before leaving home.

- Extra diapers, especially disposables
- Extra clothes, especially for different types of weather
- Extra baby wipes for diaper changes and other messes
- Extra bottles of formula and water
- Extra baby food or snacks
- Extra pacifiers and teethers
- Extra toys
- Musical tapes
- Complete first-aid kit and medications baby may be taking
- Emergency phone numbers
- Overnight equipment (if necessary) including portable crib, sleep blanket, waterproof pad, pajamas, and so on

Bonus tip: Babies need breaks while traveling, just like parents. If you're traveling by car, make frequent stops to give your baby a chance to get out of the car seat, stretch her arms and legs, and get a breath of fresh air.

192. Emergency Kit: First-Aid for Baby

Here are some items you may want to keep in your baby bag in case of an emergency.

- Digital thermometer
- Syrup of Ipecac to use if you suspect your baby has swallowed something poisonous (Use only AFTER talking to a doctor or other trained professional.)
- Acetaminophen (7 milligrams per pound of baby's body weight; can be given every four hours)
- Cough medication (over-the-counter), if prescribed by your doctor
- Nose drops, eye drops, and baby nasal spray, if prescribed by your doctor
- Band-Aids, gauze, and adhesive tape
- Measuring spoons and medicine dropper for administering medication prescribed by your doctor
- Antiseptic solution, such as hydrogen peroxide
- Nasal aspirator
- Tweezers for pulling out splinters
- Choking tube to test possible choking hazards
- Teething ointments and teethers
- Sun block
- Bug spray

Bonus tip: Create two first-aid kits, one for travel and one for home. Make sure they're easily accessible but safely out of your baby's reach.

193. Baby Gadgets: Pacifiers

Most babies require extra sucking time beyond the breast or bottle. Pacifiers, thumbs, and/or fingers can satisfy this need. Here are some facts and tips regarding pacifiers.

Try breast or bottle first. Since your baby may be hungry, the first option should be your breast or a bottle, so begin with that before inserting a pacifier.

Allow plenty of sucking time. If your baby is finished nursing and needs more sucking time, give him a pacifier or let him use his thumb or fingers.

Don't worry. There's nothing wrong with your baby sucking on a pacifier. Sucking not only satisfies a physical need, it helps your baby calm himself.

Divert your baby's attention. If you think your baby is sucking on a pacifier too often, distract him for periods of time by entertaining him with talk, games, a walk, a toy, and so on. He'll need his mouth available to explore objects in his world.

Think safety first. Make sure the pacifier is one piece, dishwasher safe, and properly sized for your baby's age. Make sure the shield is at least one and a half inches wide and made of sturdy plastic. It should also contain air holes.

Provide options. Try a variety of styles until you find the one your baby likes.

Keep it simple. Don't add honey or other additives to the pacifier. Honey contains spores that can cause botulism in babies.

No substitutions. Don't use a bottle as a pacifier.

Let your baby decide. Don't force the pacifier. Some babies never take to them. They prefer their thumbs, fingers, or nothing at all.

Caution: Never tie a pacifier to your baby's outfit. This could lead to strangulation. Instead, use a clip to attach a pacifier to your baby's clothes, so it won't get lost. Even better, keep a large supply of pacifiers on hand.

194. Quick Tip: "Losing" the Pacifier

I didn't have any problems with my baby using a pacifier. I knew he needed extra sucking time, and it was a great security for him. But when he turned two, I thought it was time to begin weaning him in preparation for preschool. I tried everything my friends recommended: putting lemon juice on it to make it taste bad, giving him a cuddly toy to hold, using stickers as a reward, but nothing worked. Eventually the pacifiers starting "disappearing" one by one. We left the last one behind at a friend's house one day, and when my baby realized it was gone, he looked at me and said, "Uh-oh." That was the end of it! I was amazed it happened so easily.

—*Jamie B.*

195. Common Concerns: Thumb Sucking

Thumb sucking soothes a distressed or anxious baby, and is a natural way for babies to comfort themselves. Babies even suck their thumbs in the womb. Most babies outgrow thumb sucking by six or seven months, if they get enough sucking time in the first weeks and months. Contrary to certain myths, thumb sucking does not cause orthodontic problems in the first two years. Here are some tips for managing thumb sucking.

- Don't use arm restraints, mittens, or bitter-tasting ointments on your baby's thumbs to prevent her from sucking.

- Offer your baby a lovey (a comfort toy to hold at night or during times of stress). The lovey may eventually replace the thumb.

- Keep your baby's hands busy with toys and other objects, and she may be less inclined to suck her thumb. This may be especially helpful when you want to wean her from thumb sucking.

196. Baby Gadgets: Teethers

Babies begin teething anywhere from three to nine months, usually around six months. Every four months or so your baby will get a few more teeth. Here are some tips to help you cope with teething.

Drooling. Excessive drooling is an early sign of teething, but it doesn't mean your baby's teeth will be coming in immediately. Some babies drool for weeks, even months, before the first tooth comes in. Wipe the drool often and use a medication if a rash develops on your baby's face. Talk to your doctor, if necessary.

Discomfort. Your baby's teeth will come in slowly as they emerge from the gum tissue. This may cause some discomfort, and your baby may fuss or cry. Topical teething medications should be used sparingly and cautiously as they can numb too large an area.

Pain. Give your baby weight-appropriate doses of acetaminophen if he develops a fever or seems to be in pain from teething. Talk to your doctor first.

Rubbing. Massage your baby's gums with your finger to soothe the pain.

Chewing. Give your baby a firm plastic teether to chew on.

Biting. Give your baby some firm teething biscuits to gnaw on. These can be very messy, but some babies find them delightful.

Chilled teethers. Chill your baby's teethers in the refrigerator or freezer to give them added soothing powers.

Bonus tip: Don't worry about crooked teeth in the first few years. They don't necessarily indicate the way your baby's permanent teeth will look.

197. Quick Tip: Frozen Foods

My baby loved teething on anything cold. I finally started freezing some of his toys, pacifiers, and teething rings. I also gave him frozen teething biscuits and fruit bits to chew on, and I filled a washcloth with ice chips and rubbed it on his gums to soothe the pain.

—Kelly S.

198. Baby Gadgets: Nose Unstuffers

If your baby has trouble clearing her nasal passages in the early weeks and months, you may have to help her out. Here are some items to keep handy.

Nasal aspirator. A small bulb syringe can be used when your baby's nose is stuffed up. Squeeze the air out of the bulb, insert the tip gently and carefully into your baby's nostril (not too far), and release the bulb slowly to suction out the mucous. Repeat with the other nostril. Rinse out the aspirator with warm water after use.

Nasal sprays. Check with your doctor before using a nasal spray. The best option for a baby is a saline solution made specifically for children. Insert the tip into your baby's nostril and spray; repeat for the other side. Don't overuse this product.

Humidifiers and vaporizers. Cool-mist humidifiers and vaporizers can play a helpful role if a room is dry or your baby is stuffy. Steam or hot-mist devices should be avoided due to the danger of scalding.

Caution: Clean your humidifier and vaporizer according to the manufacturer's instructions. Keep humidifiers and vaporizers out of the reach of children.

199. Baby Gadgets: Nail Trimmers

Babies are often born with long, soft fingernails. The nails begin to grow inside the womb, and by the time a baby is born, they can be quite long. Some nurses cover a baby's hands so she won't scratch her face with reflexive movements. However, child developmentalists believe it's better to keep your baby's hands free so she can practice eye-hand coordination and fine motor skills immediately. Trim her nails periodically to prevent her from scratching herself.

Baby nail scissors. You can buy specially designed baby scissors that make cutting your baby's nails safe and easy. Make sure the tips are rounded.

Baby nail clippers. You might try mini-nail clippers that are specially designed for babies. They're easier and safer to use than adult-size clippers. Before you clip, gently press the skin away from the nail to minimize the risk of nipping the skin.

Your teeth. Your baby's nails are soft and thin and easy to trim with your teeth. Feel free to chew them off, if nothing else works.

Bonus tip: To make the process easier, trim your baby's nails while she's asleep or after bath time—when her nails are soft. Be careful not to trim them too short. If necessary, have someone hold her while you trim her nails.

200. Baby Gadgets: Baby Carriers

Baby carriers are quite popular today, since child development experts have documented their contribution to baby's overall development. Doctors have found that babies make more rapid gains in physical growth, cognitive development, social interaction, and emotional bonding when they're worn in carriers. Here are the basic options.

Sling. A sling is an excellent carrier for newborns. It's flexible, comfortable, and molds to a parent's body easily, keeping baby snuggled and secure.

- Cost: $35 to $60
- Range: 5 to 32 pounds

Front pack. The front pack becomes an option when your baby establishes head control. You can face your baby forward to keep him entertained, or you can face him toward your body so he has better head support and can fall asleep more easily. Look for a carrier that will be comfortable for both you and your baby. It should be lightweight and provide good head support.

- Cost: $25 to $100
- Range: Up to 25 pounds

Backpack. The backpack is best for older babies who have strong head control. Look for one that offers a sturdy design, adjustable padded shoulder straps, adjustable padded hip support, and a stand-alone frame. You may need to pad the backpack to make sure your baby doesn't flop around.

- Cost: $50 to $150
- Range: 20 to 60 pounds

Safety. Make sure the carrier is well constructed, safe, and appropriate for your baby's size and developmental level.

Comfort. The carrier should be comfortable for both you and your baby. It should provide excellent support with an even distribution of your baby's weight.

Access. You should be able to get your baby in and out quickly and smoothly without hurting him.

Caution: Be careful about bending over with your baby in the carrier. You don't want to hurt your back or strain your muscles or accidentally bump your baby's head. Always be careful when moving around with your baby in the carrier. Also, don't use the carrier when doing something dangerous, such as riding a bike or riding in a car.

201. Sleeping Equipment

Bassinet or cradle. It's nice to have a specially designed bed for your baby when you first bring her home, so you can keep her near you at night, especially if you're breastfeeding. The bassinet should have a snug-fitting mattress.

- Cost: $40 to $100
- Ages: Birth to three months

Crib. To be considered safe, a crib should have narrow spaces between the slats (2⅜ inches or less), a tight-fitting mattress (no more than two finger widths between the mattress edge and crib side), short corner posts (less than 1/16 inch tall to avoid strangulation), and lead-free paint. Other options include adjustable mattress height, easy-drop side, plastic teething rail, and wheels. Never place a crib near draperies with long cords.

- Cost: $50 to $600
- Ages: Birth to three years (or until your child can climb out)

Crib mattress. If possible, buy a new mattress to make sure it's clean and safe. It should have square corners with no gaps, a waterproof cover, and ventilation holes.

- Cost: $60 to $150
- Ages: Birth to three years (or longer)

Rubber-backed sheets. You'll need at least two to keep the mattress dry if it doesn't have a waterproof covering.

Fitted crib sheets. Your baby will wet the bed no matter how many diapers you use, so it's nice to have plenty of crib sheets. Always keep a fresh one handy while the others are in the laundry. You may want to keep two sheets on the mattress, with a waterproof pad in between, so if your baby wets the bed in the middle of the night, you can simply remove the soiled sheet and pad.

Blankets. Keep several blankets of different weights on hand to keep your baby warm and comfortable.

Night-light. Plug in a night-light if your baby seems to need it to sleep.

Monitor. It lets you keep tabs on your baby while she's sleeping.

- Cost: $30 to $350
- Ages: Birth to out of crib (or longer)

Caution: Carefully examine baby equipment that's more than ten years old to make sure it meets current safety standards.

202. Equipment for Diaper Changing

Changing table. You may want to buy a table designed specifically for changing your baby's diaper. In addition to a comfortable height, make sure the table has a broad flat surface, secure base, safety belt, and washable cover.

- Cost: $90 to $500
- Ages: Birth to toilet trained

Diaper pail. Keep a diaper pail next to the changing area for easy access. Look for a pail with a lock, deodorizer, and foot pedal for easy opening.

- Cost: $15 to $30
- Ages: Birth to toilet trained

Cupboard. You may want to have a cupboard or dresser nearby to store your diaper equipment and baby clothing.

- Cost: $30 to $100
- Ages: Birth to preschool (or later)

Floor. You can always use the floor to change your baby. You won't have to worry about him rolling off and hurting himself. Line the area with waterproof sheets and blankets for protection and comfort.

Bonus tip: Changing tables today are better than ever. Many of them are sturdy units that contain lots of drawers and cubbyholes for storage. Some even come with entertainment centers.

203. Nursing Equipment

Comfortable chair. Line it with pillows and blankets for added comfort.

Rocking chair. You'll use it all the time, so make sure you find one you like. Consider a glider with a matching ottoman that also glides.

Nursing pillow. Get one that wraps around your waist to provide support for your baby while she's nursing.

Bed. You may want to put a twin bed in your baby's room, so you can both stretch out while nursing and then take a nap afterward. A twin bed may also come in handy in the middle of the night, if your baby is having trouble sleeping.

Couch. Put your legs up and relax while you nurse.

Breast pump. Expressing your breastmilk allows your partner to take a turn feeding your baby. Breast pumps also allow you to continue providing breastmilk after you return to work. Double-sided electric pumps are fast and efficient, but they're also expensive.
- Cost: $40 to $280
- Ages: Birth to weaning

Bonus tip: Keep a few items handy for added comfort, such as extra pillows, snacks, drinks, TV remote, reading material, and so on.

204. Get Up and Go: Transporting Your Baby

Infant car seats. An infant car seat should be rear-facing and specifically designed for infants only. It should have a three- or five-point harness system, multiple harness slots, detachable base, handle, adjustable straps, chest plate, washable liner, and easy-release mechanism.

- Cost: $30 to $100
- Ages: Birth to about six months or twenty pounds (models vary)

Convertible seats. When your baby has exceeded the age and weight limit for her infant car seat, she's ready to be moved to a convertible seat. Convertible seats have various harness systems and should be used rear-facing until your baby is at least one year old AND weighs twenty pounds.

- Cost: $40 to $150
- Range: 20 to 40 pounds

Caution: Make sure your baby's car seat meets current federal motor vehicle safety standards.

205. Food for Thought: Feeding Your Baby

Highchair. Your baby's highchair should have a sturdy, wide base, seat belt with crotch strap, large tray that's easy to remove, adjustable seat with removable pad, and a footrest.

- Cost: $60 to $300
- Ages: five months to two years (or later)

Booster seat. Booster seats are used as your baby gets older. They also function as highchair replacements when you're away from home. Make sure the booster seat has proper safety straps for restraining your baby and attaching to a chair.

- Cost: $30 to $50
- Ages: six months to three years (or later)

Plastic floor pad. A protective pad is nice to have if you want to keep food off the floor or carpet.

- Cost: Less than $10
- Ages: six months to teenage years!

Sippy cup. Your baby can drink by himself without spilling.

- Cost: Less than $5
- Ages: six months to three years (or later)

Suction-cup bowl and plate. These are great for your baby's first eating experiences (and beyond), since he won't be able to overturn them.

- Cost: Less than $10
- Ages: six months to three years (or later)

Plastic (or coated) spoon and fork. Look for plasticware that's specifically designed for babies, so they can feed themselves more easily.

- Cost: Less than $5
- Ages: six to eighteen months (or later)

Plastic bib. These nifty gadgets are designed with a cupped bottom to catch food as it falls while your baby is eating.

Food grinder. You won't have to buy prepared or processed baby food if you grind up your own food right from the table.

- Cost: $10 to $20
- Ages: six to eighteen months

206. Equipment for Keeping Your Baby Entertained

Baby swing. A baby swing can be a lifesaver if you have a fussy baby. It can soothe, calm, and put her to sleep. It's also good for times when you need to take an important phone call. However, don't keep your baby in the swing for long periods of time. She needs lots of exercise. Make sure your swing has sturdy legs, a wide base, a removable liner and tray, easy entry, and a safety belt.

- Cost: $60 to $130
- Ages: Depends on the model (Some provide head support for your baby. Some require your baby to be able to sit without assistance.)

Exersaucer. These "activity centers" allow your baby to bounce and swivel while playing with a variety of toys. They're great for gross and fine motor development, they're safer than jumpers and walkers, and they allow you some free time to get chores done.

- Cost: $65 to $100
- Ages: four months (when baby has good head control) to one year

Baby Jumper. This creative contraption hangs in the doorway, allowing your baby to bounce and entertain herself. Make sure the adjacent walls are three to six inches thick and the molding is firmly attached.

- Cost: $20 to $40
- Ages: four months (when baby has good head and neck control) to one year

Port-a-Crib. These are nice to have for overnight trips or naps at friends' homes. They also function as play yards to keep your baby safe and entertained while you take care of chores. Most units have a sturdy frame, locking sides, easy setup, mesh walls, side compartments, and two feet with wheels.

- Cost: $70 to $200
- Ages: Birth to two years (or later)

Caution: Although babies love portable walkers on wheels, they're no longer considered safe. Babies can be injured by tipping over or falling down stairs. Also, walkers may interfere with crawling, an important developmental milestone.

207. Strollers and Infant Seats

Stroller. Umbrella strollers are lightweight and portable, but they don't have much storage. Regular strollers offer more comfort, storage, and seat positions for your baby. Many include a removable hood, washable liner, and beverage holders. Make sure your stroller has a seat belt, crotch strap, swivel wheels, wheel locks, tall handles, and a footrest. Three-wheeled jogging strollers are also available for exercising with your baby or walking on dirt paths.

- Cost: $30 to $400
- Ages: Birth to four years (or later)

Infant seats. These allow your baby to be propped up so he can see more easily. They're NEVER to be used as car seats. Many infant seats are lightweight and sturdy. Make sure your infant seat has a seat belt with crotch strap. Some have removable liners and vibrators for added convenience and comfort.

- Cost: $30 to $100
- Ages: Birth to nine months (or later)

Caution: If you're borrowing or buying secondhand equipment, make sure it's in good condition and meets federal safety standards. If you have questions, contact the Consumer Product Safety Commission at 800-638-CPSC or www.cpsc.gov.

208. Store That Stuff: Storage

Store it. Consider storing your baby's clothing and equipment in a chest of drawers, a cupboard, or several large bins or plastic containers.

Lock it. Lock up all dangerous items and store them in a safe place.

Shelve it. Low-lying shelves give your baby access to clothing, toys, stuffed animals, and other playthings. Shelves also make cleanup easier. Make sure all items on the shelves are safe for your baby.

Chapter 12:
Baby's Physical Development

209. Growing Gains: Physical Development

Your baby makes rapid gains in physical development over the first year (the second fastest growth period after prenatal development). Here are some facts and tips.

Birth weight. Most babies weigh between six and nine pounds at birth, about the same weight as a gallon of milk. The weight is mostly in the form of fat for insulation and nutrition storage. Babies lose between five and ten percent of their birth weight after delivery, and gain it back within the first two weeks of life. This is normal.

Weight doubles. Your baby's weight will double by the end of the first four months. Babies need primarily breastmilk or formula in the first several months. They aren't ready for solid food until four to six months.

Weight triples. By the end of the first year, your baby will triple her birth weight as her bones, muscles, and organs continue to grow. The average baby weighs twenty-two pounds at twelve months. By her first birthday, your baby should be eating plenty of solid foods including cereals, fruits, and vegetables.

Birth length. Most babies measure between eighteen and twenty-two inches at birth, about the distance from your elbow to your fingertips. Your baby's height is primarily determined by genetics, but a good diet will help ensure that she reaches her potential.

Growth. Babies grow about an inch a month and measure about thirty inches at the end of the first year. By two years your baby will reach about half her adult height.

Head. Babies' heads measure about a fourth of their body length at birth, while adults' heads measure only an eighth of body length. Don't worry, your baby's head doesn't shrink. Her body just catches up.

Legs. Babies' legs measure about a fourth of their body length at birth, while adults' legs measure half of body length. Let your baby practice standing on her legs to help them grow straight and strong. Ignore the old wives' tale that if you let your baby bear weight on her legs, she'll become bowlegged.

Feet. Surprisingly, your baby's feet will be five times larger by the time she's an adult! Don't panic. It doesn't happen all at once. Your baby doesn't need shoes during the first year of life, except for warmth or decoration. Let her go barefoot as much as possible.

Bonus tip: If your baby looks healthy overall, she probably is. Don't be obsessive about weighing her as long as she appears to be in good physical shape and developing well. Make sure she's producing eight to twelve wet diapers a day.

Caution: Don't put your baby on a diet if you think she's overweight. Check with your doctor about feeding recommendations. Your baby will most likely outgrow her chubbiness as her height increases.

210. Large Muscle Movement: Arms, Legs, and Body

Gross motor movement involves large body parts such as the head, torso, arms, and legs. Your baby makes rapid gains in gross motor development during the first year. Here's a general look at the gross motor milestones and some tips for enhancing your baby's development. Keep in mind that there's a wide range of normal in these areas. Talk to your doctor if you're worried that your baby may be delayed.

Two to three months. Your baby may lift his head from the floor while lying on his stomach. Lie down on the floor and show him a toy to encourage him to lift his head.

Three to six months. Your baby may roll over. You can help him practice rolling over by placing him on his stomach, tucking one arm at his side, and gently rolling him over.

Four to five months. Your baby may lift himself up on his arms and push his legs to inch his body forward. Lay him on his stomach and prop a towel under his chest to help him practice moving his arms and legs. Place your hands on his feet so he can push off.

Four to seven months. Your baby may sit propped up. If he has trouble sitting, add extra props so he's well supported. Put him in his infant seat or car seat so he can see the world from a sitting position.

Five to seven months. Your baby may sit up by himself. Help him practice by putting him in a sitting position (legs crossed) and supporting his back with your hands. Then let go for a few seconds.

Five to eight months. Your baby may master the belly crawl (also called creeping) by dragging his stomach on the ground as he moves forward. Place a toy a few inches from his grasp so he's motivated to creep forward and reach the toy.

Six to ten months. Your baby may stand holding on to something. Help him practice by grasping both of his hands and holding him in a standing position.

Eight to ten months. Your baby may lift his stomach from the floor and crawl, alternating his arms and legs. Put a toy a few inches away and place him on his stomach. Lift his stomach off the floor, leaving his knees and hands on the floor, and encourage him to move forward to get the toy.

211. More on Large Muscle Movement

Nine to twelve months. Your baby may walk awkwardly while holding your hands. Hold her hands securely while she's standing, and lean forward so she has to move a foot forward to support her weight.

Ten to twelve months. Your baby may stand alone momentarily. Hold her hands while she's standing, slowly remove one hand from her grasp, then remove the other hand if she's stable. Be there to spot her if she starts to fall.

Eleven to thirteen months. Your baby may stand alone for several seconds. Place her near a piece of furniture, give her a toy to hold, and encourage her to let go of the furniture as she concentrates on the toy.

Eleven to fourteen months. Your baby may "cruise" (walk while holding on to furniture). Place a toy on one end of the couch, place your baby at the other end, and encourage her to move down the couch to get the toy.

Eleven to fifteen months. Your baby may walk unassisted. Hold her hands, encourage her to take a step, then carefully let go. Spot her in case she starts to fall.

Mobility. Mobility changes your baby's life. Once she starts crawling and walking, there's no stopping her. Walking enhances many aspects of your baby's development, including fine motor skills (hands and fingers), cognitive ability, and social awareness. While she's walking, she'll hold objects, think about where she's going, and check in with you for reassurance. Be aware of new dangers as your baby begins to crawl and eventually walk, and make sure to childproof your home before she gets moving. It's amazing how quickly she can get into danger. (See pages 310–318.)

Developmental differences. Some babies walk as early as nine months, although they appear bowlegged, flatfooted, and unbalanced. Others may not walk until eighteen months or beyond. Your baby will walk when she's ready. There's no correlation between when a baby walks and how intelligent or physically capable she is. If you're concerned about your baby's gross motor development, check with your doctor.

212. Small Muscle Movement: Hands, Fingers, Feet, and Toes

Fine motor movements involve smaller body parts such as hands, fingers, feet, and toes. Here are some facts and tips about fine motor development.

One to three months. Your baby may wave at an object in an attempt to touch or grab it. Place a toy or colorful object within your baby's visual range (about eight to twelve inches from his face), and watch him try to grasp it.

Two to three months. Your baby may touch an object and reflexively grasp it if it's placed in his hand. Find a graspable toy, such as a rattle or teething ring, and brush it against your baby's hand so he can wrap his fingers around it.

Three to four months. Your baby may try to grasp an object with his whole hand and palm. Sometimes he'll succeed; sometimes he won't. Hold a toy within his visual range and encourage him to grasp it.

Four to eight months. Your baby may transfer an object from one hand to the other. Place a toy in one of his hands, then offer another toy to the same hand. He might transfer the first toy to the other hand so he can grasp the new toy.

Five to six months. Your baby may reach for, grasp at, and hold on to an object. He may also shake a rattle, hold a bottle, and pull on your hair. Offer him a variety of objects so he can practice holding different things.

Eight to ten months. Your baby may try to catch something tossed at him, but he probably won't be able to make contact. Seat him on the floor and roll a ball toward him. See if he reaches for it. Try tossing a soft stuffed animal at his hands (being careful not to hit his face.)

Nine to twelve months. Your baby may master picking up objects with his thumb and forefinger (pincer grasp). Place small frozen peas or Cheerios on his highchair tray, and let him practice picking them up.

Eleven to twelve months. Your baby may use both hands to hold a larger object. Give him a large, lightweight toy that requires two hands to hold, such as a ball or stuffed animal. See what he does with it.

Exploration. When your baby learns to grasp objects, he'll begin exploring them by putting them in his mouth. Oral exploration provides information on taste, size, temperature, softness, texture, and so on.

Back and tummy time. Let your child spend time on his back to develop his fine motor skills. Give him time on his stomach to develop his gross motor skills.

Caution: Constantly monitor your child's play areas for choking hazards. If it's small enough to fit into a toilet paper roll, it's a choking hazard.

213. Baby Games: Stimulating Baby's Physical Development

Enhance your baby's body awareness and motor skills through fun games and activities.

Massage. Physical touch is great for enhancing body awareness.

Tootsie roll. Lay your baby on a towel or blanket and help her roll over.

Boat ride. Place your baby on a blanket or towel and pull her around the room.

Sponge. Have your baby squeeze a sponge to enhance her fine motor skills.

Laundry. Let your baby climb around in the laundry pile to experience various textures, colors, and fabrics.

Tunnel crawl. Cut the ends off a cardboard box and encourage your baby to crawl through.

Baby ball. Place your baby on her stomach on a large beach ball, and gently roll her around while holding her hands.

Chapter 13:
Baby's Cognitive Development

214. Baby's Cognitive Development

Your baby's cognitive development begins at birth, and perhaps even before, according to many child developmentalists. Here are some facts and tips regarding your baby's cognitive development.

Active learning. Your baby needs to interact with his environment in order to learn about it. He participates in his own education by using his senses. Let him explore his world through sight, hearing, taste, touch, and smell.

Preferences. Your baby develops preferences for certain experiences such as playing Pat-a-Cake or taking a bath, and he loves repetition. At the same time, he enjoys the novelty of new experiences, so offer him plenty of sensory stimulation and introduce him to lots of new games.

Selectivity. Your baby receives the same input as everyone else, but he perceives it differently based on his innate abilities, experiences, and developmental level. Perception is your baby's way of selectively interacting with all the possibilities in his environment. Watch how he responds to different kinds of light, such as bright and dim, and different sounds such as loud and soft.

Organization. Your baby begins to organize his world through repeated interaction with his environment. Even though he doesn't have words for such concepts as soft, hard, big, and small, he's already beginning to understand these concepts by using his senses. Give him the words for objects and concepts as he comes into contact with them, and soon he'll understand their meaning.

Memory. Your baby's memory is central to cognitive development. Young babies can remember objects for only a few seconds or minutes. By six months, a baby's ability to remember objects extends to a week or two, if he's given a chance to interact with the objects frequently. Show your baby a toy, then show it to him again a few hours later. Watch his response. Wait a day before showing him the same toy, and see if he remembers it.

Reading. It's never too early to read to your baby. Some parents read to their babies while they're still in the womb. Simple books with rhyming words and colorful illustrations are best.

Cause and effect. Your baby begins to understand cause and effect in the first few days of life. This ability to understand reactions eventually leads to a more sophisticated cognitive skill: problem solving. Push a button on his busy box and watch his reaction. Soon he'll be pushing the button himself.

215. Cognitive Milestones

By six months your baby can categorize objects based on their shape, color, density, size, and number up to three. Name these objects for your baby so she can begin to learn the terms.

By nine months your baby can discern different faces, animals, and objects, even ones in photographs. Show your baby pictures in baby books and talk about their differences.

By one year your baby can generalize memories and use them in various ways. For example, she can take a new toy that resembles an old toy and use it the same way. Show your baby a set of blocks that are similar to but different from a familiar set of blocks, and see how she responds.

Bonus tip: YOU are the best plaything for your baby. You stimulate her senses and increase her cognitive development through frequent interaction. By simply playing with your baby, you're helping her become smarter, happier, and more physically fit.

Caution: Babies who don't have the opportunity to interact with their environment may experience developmental delays. Don't overprotect your baby by limiting her exposure to the world. Make sure her environment is safe, then let her explore it.

216. Language Milestones

At birth. Your baby's first language is crying. She also imitates your facial expressions early on, so make faces at her and watch her try to copy you.

One to two months. Your baby produces a wide range of meaningful noises such as cooing, fussing, laughing, and crying. Make funny noises for her to imitate, and copy the ones she makes.

Three to six months. Your baby starts to experiment with new sounds such as squeals, growls, croons, "motorboats," and vowels. Continue making different noises for her to try, and copy the ones she makes.

Six to ten months. Your baby begins to babble by repeating various vowels and consonant-vowel combinations. Repeating sounds such as ba-ba-ba and goo-goo-goo helps her learn the consonant-vowel combinations that make up various words.

Ten to twelve months. Your baby begins to understand simple words such as *juice, dada, doggy, up,* and *more.* Some babies understand twenty-five words or simple phrases by the end of the first year. Repeat familiar words several times so your baby can absorb them, and keep your sentences short and simple.

Twelve to thirteen months. Your baby's first word will probably be one that's important to her, such as *dada* (which is easier to say than *mama*). Give her lots of input, and soon she'll be saying all kinds of words.

217. Baby Talk: Language and Communication

A baby's language development begins at birth. By the time he reaches one year, he'll probably have mastered his first word. However, long before he says his first official word, he's already "talking" in his own way. If you pay close attention, you'll be able to understand most of his gestures, sounds, and attempts at speech. Here are some facts and tips about language development.

Preferences. Your baby prefers hearing speech to other sounds in his environment. He has an innate interest in your voice and finds it fascinating. Chat with him throughout the day, and vary your voice from time to time to make it even more fun to listen to.

Positive reinforcement. Babies learn language partly through a predisposition for it and partly through experiences and reinforcement. When your baby makes a sound, give him positive reinforcement by repeating the sound, smiling at him, and encouraging him to make more sounds.

Baby talk. Babies love baby talk, and it's fun for parents, too. Your child won't be using baby talk when he gets to high school (unless he's babysitting a young child), so don't worry about him not learning the proper way to speak. Enjoy the sounds of language, model the correct forms, and eventually he'll do the same.

Parent talk. Sometimes called Motherese or Parentese, parent talk is a natural, almost subconscious way of teaching your baby to talk. Babies prefer high-pitched voices, varied intonation, short simple sentences, repetition, questions, simple commands, facial expressions, and body language. Keep this in mind while talking to your baby.

Caution: Don't correct your baby's attempts at speech, or he may become self-conscious and slow down or stop his language development. Model the precise sounds and correct forms of language by using them everyday, and eventually he'll learn them. If you're worried about your baby's speech, talk to your doctor about consulting a speech therapist or other specialist.

218. Quick Tip: No!

I try not to say no too much to my baby. I don't want it to be the first word out of his mouth when he finally begins talking. Instead of saying, "No, don't play with that," I try to say something positive such as, "Let's play with this toy." I use no only when it's a dangerous situation, so he'll know the word is important.

—Connie P.

219. Baby Games: Stimulating Baby's Brain

Spending time with your baby is the best way to stimulate her cognitive development. Enjoy your time together with songs, games, activities, and conversation. Here are a few tips to get you started.

Peek-a-Boo. Play this old favorite to enhance your baby's language development, social interactions, and understanding of cause and effect. Begin by covering your face with a cloth, saying, "Where's mommy?" and removing the cloth. Watch her face light up.

Pat-a-Cake. This classic hand game will help increase your baby's language skills, cognitive abilities, and eye-hand coordination.

Where's-Baby's-Toy? Hide a toy under a cloth, then ask your baby where the toy is. After a few seconds, pull off the cloth and show her the toy. Repeat several times.

Mouth Music. Make funny sounds with your mouth, and repeat them over and over so your baby has a chance to practice her speech skills.

Bells-on-Her-Toes. Attach a belled bracelet to your baby's wrist or ankle, and let her try to figure out how to make the sound. This helps develop her problem-solving abilities and understanding of cause and effect.

Play Puppet. Have a chat with your baby using a puppet. This helps enhance her language skills, cognitive development, and social interaction.

What Happened? Build a block tower, then let your baby knock it over. She'll learn more about cause and effect, spatial relationships, and motor skills.

Baby's Body. Get a mirror and ask your baby where her nose is. Point to it and repeat the word several times. Then add new body parts to help her learn vocabulary, self-awareness, and motor skills.

Bang-a-Drum. Give your baby a wooden stick and some pans or bowls to pound on. Watch as she begins to increase her motor abilities, understanding of cause and effect, and thinking skills.

220. Quick Tip: Food Art

When I'm preparing food such as spaghetti sauce or a jelly sandwich, I always put a little glob on my baby's highchair tray so he can explore it and enjoy it in his own way. Mostly he makes a mess, but he loves experiencing new sensations. Cleaning the mess is a small price to pay for the joy of watching him learn about new tastes and textures.

—Holly K.

Chapter 14:
Baby's Emotional Development

221. Mad, Sad, or Glad: Expressing Emotions

In the past, psychologists believed that babies had no real emotions at birth. We now know that a newborn exhibits a wide range of emotions after delivery. These partly reflexive, partly emotional expressions help to shape the reactions of the people around her. As you begin to recognize your baby's signals, you'll be better able to respond to them quickly and appropriately. Here are some emotional signals you may recognize in your baby and tips for how to respond to them.

Distress. This is one of the most common emotions you'll see. Distress can be caused by physical discomfort, hunger, a lack of support from caregivers, or a startling surprise such as a loud noise or an object coming too near her face. Your baby will signal distress by crying, an indication that she needs to be comforted. If you respond quickly and consistently, your baby will learn that you'll be there for her and that she can rely on you to take care of her. Pick her up when she cries, and she'll cry less by the end of the first year. Ignore what others may say about spoiling your baby. Babies cannot be spoiled in the first year.

Sadness. Babies may exhibit sensitivity to others' sad feelings by fussing or crying when another baby or parent cries. Babies of depressed mothers tend to imitate the facial expressions of sadness, as if they're empathizing with their mothers. Try to keep a pleasant look on your face, so your baby will respond in kind.

Interest/Excitement. Your baby may appear wide-eyed and alert when something catches her attention. She may try to make eye contact or stare at an object. She may even try to follow an object if you're moving it in front of her, so move it slowly and watch how she responds.

Contentment. Your baby experiences a feeling of pleasure when she's content, satisfied, cuddled, held, or attended to. Although some experts say that babies don't really smile until six to eight weeks, you might perceive your baby smiling soon after birth. Someone else might call it gas, but you may sense that your baby's smile is a response to all the smiles you're giving her. If she's not smiling yet, just keep smiling at her and she'll soon smile back.

Joy. By two or three months your baby may chortle or even laugh in response to your games and silly faces. She may also laugh while entertaining herself with a rattle or other fun toy. Laugh with your baby, give her plenty of smiles, make funny faces, and play games with her. Soon she'll be giggling, too.

Anger/Frustration. By three months your baby may experience frustration at not being able to control a situation or get what she wants. She may cry and exhibit tantrum-like behavior. By six months she may direct her anger toward someone or something specific, and express her frustration through body language, facial expressions, and tears. Soothe your baby when she's upset, reassure her with your voice and touch, give her the words for her feelings, and understand that she's expressing a normal human emotion.

222. More on Expressing Emotions

Fear. Soon after birth, your baby may express a fear-like reaction when something startles him. However, real fears grow over time, peaking around nine to fourteen months. As your baby begins to understand his world, he may begin to experience a fear of the dark or of men with beards. Reassure him, make him feel safe and secure, and let him know you're always there for him.

Stranger Anxiety. Your baby may develop a fear of strangers around six to eight months, peaking around one year. Some babies don't exhibit stranger anxiety at all; they happily socialize with just about anyone. Other babies respond to strangers by being slow to warm up. Some babies may be afraid of certain visual characteristics such as beards, glasses, hats, or masks. Ease your baby gently into situations with strangers, and let him get acquainted at his own pace.

Separation Anxiety. Between nine and eighteen months, many babies fear being left by their mothers, fathers, or other primary caregivers. Separation anxiety peaks around one year. Many psychologists believe that babies fear abandonment at this stage. They don't realize that when their mother disappears for a few minutes, she will eventually reappear. You can help your baby overcome these insecurities by talking to him when you leave the room, reassuring him that you're still nearby, and hurrying back whenever possible.

223. Quick Tip: Fussy Time

Most of the mothers in my mother's group complained about having trouble getting dinner ready because their babies often got fussy at dinnertime. I told them my trick. I'd put my baby down on the kitchen floor with cups, bowls, pots, pans, and Cheerios to play with. While he kept busy "cooking," I was able to get dinner started without a lot of fuss.

—Susan W.

224. Watch My Face: Social Referencing

A baby's understanding of her emotions is partly influenced by the reactions of people around her. For example, imagine that your baby bumps her head. You can react three ways. You can panic by frantically running to her, picking her up, and saying, "Poor baby!" You can ignore it, tell her she's fine, and walk away. Or you can react calmly, watch your baby's reaction, and intervene if she needs your assistance. All three are examples of social referencing. The wait-and-see method works best because it allows your baby to respond to her own feelings instead of responding to yours. Here are some tips for stimulating and reacting to your baby's emotions.

Imitation. If you cry, your baby is likely to cry, too. If you smile, your baby will probably do the same. Sit with your baby in your lap, facing you, and encourage her to imitate your facial expressions, body language, and tone of voice. This will help her learn more about expressing her feelings.

Encouragement. You can use social referencing to encourage your child to try new things. For example, if you want her to try a new food, then smile and make yummy noises while tasting it in front of her.

Caution: Try to avoid displaying disgust at things that bother you, such as bugs, dirty diapers, or strong smelling foods. Your baby may learn to imitate your emotions instead of experiencing her own.

225. Baby Love: Cuddling with Baby

Cuddling, holding, and nurturing your baby are just as important as feeding, changing, and clothing her. Studies have shown that premature babies who were held a lot in the nursery made greater and faster advances than babies who were not held for long periods of time. Smile at your baby, make eye contact, chat with her, and hold her as much and as long as you like. Some of the benefits of cuddling include a strong attachment, enhanced development, increased contentment, and a sense of security. Here are some ways to cuddle with your baby.

- Wear your baby in a front pack or sling.
- Carry your baby in a football hold (across your forearm).
- Place your baby in your lap.
- Rock your baby.
- Dance with your baby.
- Lie in bed with your baby on your chest.
- Give your baby a massage.
- Hold your baby close to your face and softly sing to her.
- Snuggle with your baby in a soft blanket.
- Hold your baby in a comfortable chair with lots of pillows.
- Let your baby play with your hair.
- Take your baby in the bath with you.

226. Quick Tip:
A Hundred Kisses

I try to give my baby a hundred kisses a day. On his face, head, arms, legs, tummy, back, hands, and feet. I love it when he smiles and laughs when I kiss him, and it's so cute when he tries to kiss me back. I highly recommend a hundred kisses a day.

—Mia T.

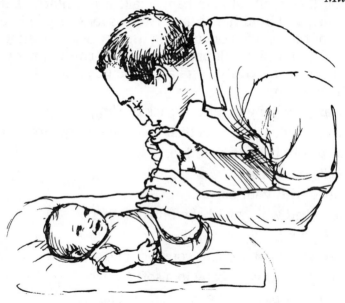

Chapter 15:
Baby's Psychological Development

227. All About Me: Psychological Development

The development of a baby's personality is influenced by both her genetic predisposition and her interaction with the world.

Self-awareness. As your baby grows and develops, she becomes more aware of herself as an individual. Once she realizes she's separate from her mother, she becomes egocentric, which means she believes the world revolves around her. This emerging self-awareness is not selfishness, however. It's an important developmental milestone that helps your baby gain the confidence she needs to succeed later in life. Set up a mirror so your baby can start to recognize what she looks like.

Mine! If your baby grabs a toy away from another baby, it means she has learned a sense of ownership. Help her learn to share by providing enough toys for everyone, and allow her to have a few special toys all to herself.

My body! As your baby learns more about her body, she gains a greater sense of self and an increased understanding of her physical abilities. She'll be especially fascinated with her face, since it's familiar, expressive, and entertaining to her. Play games that incorporate her body parts, such as Peek-a-Boo, Pat-a-Cake, and Head-Shoulders-Knees-and-Toes.

My name! Your baby's name is also important to her self-awareness. Use it frequently so she can learn to recognize it.

228. Watch Me!: Personality

Personality is defined as the collection of emotions, temperament, behaviors, and attitudes that make each person an individual. Here are five basic personality traits and tips on how to manage them.

Extroverted. An extroverted baby tends to be outgoing, assertive, and active. She'll probably need extra guidance and control as she grows.

Agreeable. An agreeable baby tends to be kind, helpful, and easygoing. She may be easy to overlook, so make sure she gets the attention she needs.

Conscientious. A conscientious baby tends to be organized, deliberate, and conforming. She prefers structure and stability, and she needs help becoming more flexible.

Neurotic. A neurotic baby tends to be anxious, moody, and self-punishing. She needs a lot of encouragement, self-esteem enhancement, and gentle responses.

Open. An open baby tends to be imaginative, curious, artistic, and welcoming of new experiences. Provide her with a wide range of opportunities.

Bonus tip: Erik Eriksson, a well-known child developmentalist, believed that infancy is a period of gaining trust with the environment. The more parents respond to their baby's needs, the more trusting the baby will be.

229. Born to Be Wild?: Baby's Temperament

Babies are born with certain behavioral tendencies that remain relatively constant throughout life. You may be able to recognize the following dimensions of temperament in your baby as early as a few weeks old.

Activity level. Some babies are very active and need lots of opportunities to release energy. Other babies are less active and need encouragement to engage in active play.

Rhythm. Some babies eat, sleep, and defecate on schedule almost from birth. Other babies are much less predictable. If your baby is very regular, he needs the security of staying on schedule. If he's irregular, you might need to be flexible to help him get used to a routine.

Approach/withdrawal. Some babies delight in new experiences while others withdraw from new situations. If your baby enjoys new things, keep an eye on him so he doesn't get into trouble. If he tends to withdraw, ease him into new situations without forcing him to participate.

Adaptability. Some babies adjust quickly to change; others are unhappy at every disruption of their routine. If your baby adapts well, he'll be fairly easy to handle. If he doesn't adapt well, you'll need to encourage him, let him move at his own pace, and give him the opportunity to make choices.

Intensity of reaction. Some babies chortle and howl; others respond with a smile or a whimper. If your baby reacts intensely, try to soothe him, but don't stifle him. If he's quiet, encourage him to express himself.

Threshold of responsiveness. Some babies sense every sight, sound, and touch; others seem blissfully unaware of bright lights, loud noises, or wet diapers. If your baby is very sensitive, he'll need periods of quiet to unwind. If he doesn't seem particularly sensitive to sensory stimulation, help him become more aware of the sights and sounds in his environment.

Quality of mood. Some babies are constantly happy, smiling at almost everything; others are ready to protest at any moment. If you have a happy baby, enjoy his pleasant moods but watch him closely for signs of unhappiness (in case he's subtle about showing these emotions). If he's generally cranky, understand his disposition and encourage him to express himself more positively.

Distractibility. All babies fuss when they're hungry, but some will stop if someone gives them a pacifier or sings them a song. If your baby is easily distracted, it'll be easier for you to move him away from dangerous situations. If he's not easily distracted, you'll have to work harder to redirect his attention.

Attention span. Some babies play happily with one toy for a long time; others become bored quickly. If your baby has a long attention span, he'll play on his own for long periods of time. If he has a short attention span, you may have to provide lots of entertainment.

230. Temperament Types

Easy/good. Forty percent of babies are considered "easy" or "good." They have regular habits, relaxed attitudes, a generally happy disposition, good distractibility, and a low threshold of responsiveness. If you have such a baby, count your blessings.

Slow to warm up/shy. Fifteen percent of babies are considered "slow to warm up" or "shy." They're initially unwilling to approach new situations and have trouble adapting. They usually adjust over time, but at their own pace. Encourage your shy baby to engage in new experiences, but don't push her or shame her for being shy.

Difficult. Ten percent of babies are considered "difficult." They tend to have irregular habits, intense emotional reactions, a generally unhappy disposition, poor distractibility, and a high threshold of responsiveness. They're challenging to live with and require extra care and patience when being moved from one activity to another.

Mixed temperament. Thirty-five percent of babies don't fit neatly into the above categories. Be flexible with your baby and be prepared to roll with her mood swings.

Bonus tip: Your baby's temperament will remain essentially the same throughout her life, but it can be changed somewhat by environmental circumstances or inner resolve. You can help a shy child become more outgoing, and you can calm a difficult child through sensitive, effective parenting.

Chapter 16:
Baby's Social Development

231. You're My Best Friend: Social Development

Your baby's social development begins before birth as he listens to your muted voice and feels your gentle massage. Here are some ways your baby bonds with you, and some tips for forming a lifelong attachment.

Hormones. During and after childbirth, a mother releases hormones that play a role in triggering maternal feelings. She often experiences intense emotion right after the birth, which helps her bond with her baby. Don't be afraid to express your emotions, both positive and negative, to your family, friends, and medical support staff.

Premature babies. Pre-term babies who are handled by their parents and nurses make more rapid gains in all areas of development. Touching and holding your premature baby (often called kangaroo care) will help form a close bond.

Baby care. While it's important to hold your baby right after birth, it's really the long-term, day-to-day care that ensures a close relationship.

Caution: Postpartum depression can interfere with bonding between a mother and her baby. A mother may feel exhausted, sad, inadequate, and overwhelmed. Many new mothers experience varying degrees of postpartum depression. If you feel depressed, talk to your doctor. You may need medical treatment.

232. We Are Family: Parent and Child Connection

The match between parent and child is called "goodness of fit." No matter what your temperaments or personality types are, you can have a harmonious relationship with your child. However, you may have to adapt your parenting techniques to achieve this.

Synchrony. You and your baby are "in sync" when you can read each other's cues and respond appropriately. Watch your baby, listen to his sounds, observe his body language, identify his needs, and respond appropriately.

Sensitivity. If you're sensitive to your baby's basic needs, you'll be better able to respond to his signals. In addition to food, warmth, clean diapers, and a bed, your baby needs attention, love, and physical contact.

Contact. If you share time with your baby by holding him, talking to him, playing with him, and watching him, you're helping to ensure an excellent fit.

Caregiving. Be consistent and conscientious about your baby's care. Make sure he has clean diapers, good food, a quiet place to sleep, and so on.

Attachment. Your baby will show his attachment by wanting to be close to you. Later, he'll use you as a security base as he begins to explore his world. Let him be with you as much as he needs to be. A strong attachment to you will help ensure that he has healthy relationships later in life.

233. Play Time: Types of Social Play

Through social play, a child learns important skills such as cooperation, sharing, joining groups, making and keeping friends, and so on. These skills don't develop until the preschool years, but it's important to set a positive tone for healthy, happy social play while your baby is young. Here's an overview of the different stages of play your baby will go through in the first few years, along with tips for enhancing her social development.

Solitary play. In the first level of play, your baby plays alone even if there are other babies present. She's essentially in her own world, oblivious to others around her. Allow your child to enjoy solitary play by providing toys she can use to master skills and solve problems. (See Chapter 17.)

Onlooker play. In the next level of play, your child watches other children play but doesn't participate physically because she may be slow to warm up, unfamiliar with the children, or she may prefer watching. Although she's not participating physically, she's "playing" inside her mind. In other words, she's imagining that she's playing with the other kids, and she may even act out the play later on when the kids are gone. Allow her to watch other kids play without forcing her to participate. She's enjoying herself.

Parallel play. Your child plays next to another child, perhaps with similar toys, but doesn't interact with the child in a meaningful way. She is, however, enjoying the other child's company.

Associative play. Your child interacts with other children and shares materials, but she still plays her own way. There's no shared or common goal. Try not to interfere with her play. Allow her to try out new roles and play the way she wants, as long as she's not disrupting other children or violating established rules.

234. Play and Learn: How Your Baby Learns through Play

Sensory-motor play. Your baby uses his senses and physical skills to splash in the tub, pour sand, roll down a grassy hill, and so on. Provide him with lots of opportunities to use his senses and motor skills in play.

Mastery play. Your baby works on mastering a task such as putting together nesting bowls, climbing a step, or doing a simple puzzle. Give him lots of manipulative toys so he can practice mastery play.

Rough-and-tumble play. Roughhousing is usually more common among boys (and dads) than girls. As your child engages in roughhousing, he may look intense, fearful, even angry, but this is his "play face," an expression of his enjoyment. Allow him to express his emotions and release his energy through rough-and-tumble play, but always be careful so he doesn't get hurt.

235. Quick Tip: Where's Mommy?

Lie down on the floor and cover yourself up with a blanket, in plain view of your baby. Make noises from under the blanket. If your baby is around eight or nine months, he'll try to find you. If he's younger, you may have to peek out from under the blanket to help him find you.

—Vicki S.

236. Playmates: Interacting with Baby

Your baby can engage in social play from day one. All he needs is you.

Baby massage. Give your baby a massage using baby lotion. Sing or talk about your baby's different body parts as you caress him all over.

Finger Face. Draw a face on your hand, and talk with your baby using your hand as a chatty pal.

Gotcha Glove. Decorate a glove with lots of colored markers to make a funny face, then have the glove "creep" toward your baby. Say, "Gotcha!" when the glove makes contact.

Hats Off. Put on a funny hat and let your baby pull it off. Replace the hat and play again. Occasionally surprise him with a new hat.

Pop-Goes-the-Parent. Get a large box, hide inside, then pop out and surprise your baby. Just don't scare him too much!

Whoopsy Daisy. Stack a bunch of blocks, then let your baby knock them over!

Bonus tip: Just about anything you do while interacting with your baby will entertain him. Don't worry about having a lot of special toys and games. You (and that funny face of yours) are his most important toys.

237. Duets: Talking with Your Baby

Here are some tips for communicating with your baby.

Eye contact. Get your baby's attention by looking at her. Position yourself about eight to twelve inches from her face. Your eyes are naturally attractive to your baby, so let them begin the conversation.

Soft voice. Use a soft, slightly higher pitched voice to attract your baby's attention. Make your voice interesting by varying the pitch occasionally.

Baby's name. Use your baby's name often, and she'll soon learn to respond to it. Call her by name to attract her attention to your conversation.

Short sentences. Keep your sentences simple, clear, and concrete, so your baby can receive and eventually understand your messages more easily.

Feedback. Give your baby positive reinforcement when she attempts to speak, and soon she'll be repeating sounds and syllables. Never correct her speech. Just model the appropriate language.

Simple questions. When you talk to your baby, ask simple questions, then give her time to "respond." Watch her move her mouth, make sounds, or move her body in rhythm to your conversation. Imitate her responses.

Repetition. Repeat words when talking to your baby, and she'll soon learn them.

Facial expression. Enhance your words by using appropriate facial expressions and body language.

Singing. Sing to your baby, read her stories, make funny noises, and show her all the ways to enjoy her voice.

238. *Quick Tip: Dancing Baby*

Whenever the spirit moved me, I turned on music and started dancing with my baby. I sang songs to him while dancing, which he seemed to enjoy more than regular holding or rocking. The music held his attention, and each time the song changed, we changed the dance. He started doing his own dancing when he learned to stand up.

—Simonie W.

239. *Quick Tip:* Pat the Bunny

My baby loved the book Pat the Bunny. *I read it to him every night, beginning with the first night home from the hospital. I helped him gently stroke the soft fur. He really seemed to respond to that book. He's three now, and we still read* Pat the Bunny *and* Goodnight Moon *every night.*

—Holly K.

240. Say It with Signs: Baby Sign Language

Using sign language with babies is becoming popular with parents as a way of encouraging communication and overall language development. You can buy a book that shows you simple baby signs, or you can make up your own gestures. Here are some common signs to use with your baby, taken from American Sign Language.

Hi. Raise your open hand up, and wave it back and forth.

Bye-bye. Wave good-bye by opening and closing your hand.

Drink. Gesture holding a cup and pouring a drink into your mouth.

Milk. Squeeze your hand open and closed into a fist, as if milking a cow.

Eat. Bring your fingertips together and tap your mouth several times.

Cookie. Pretend to cut out a cookie on your palm with your fingertips.

Up. Point up with your index finger.

Down. Point down with your index finger.

Bedtime. Put your palms together and place your hands on the side of your face to make a pillow.

Mommy. Open your hand and tap the tip of your thumb on your chin several times.

Daddy. Open your hand and tap the tip of your thumb on your forehead several times.

Baby. Cradle one arm in the other, and rock them back and forth as if rocking a baby.

Dog. Pat your leg as if calling a dog, or snap your thumb against your middle finger.

Play. Stick out your thumbs and pinky fingers on both hands, tuck in your other fingers, then rotate your hands back and forth at the wrists.

More. Make an O with each hand by touching your fingertips to your thumbtip. Tap your hands together at the fingertips several times.

Want. Reach out with both hands open and palms facing up, then bring your hands toward your body while closing your fingers into claw shapes.

Go. Point your index fingers in the direction you want to go.

Book. Hold your flat hands together, then open them like a book.

241. Quick Tip: Box of Baby

Every time we got a new appliance, we kept the box for a few days. We made sure all the staples and other dangerous items were removed. Our baby just loved to sit inside. If it was a big box, we'd cut holes in it so she could see out. Sometimes we'd cover it with a light blanket and play peek-a-boo. I think playing in the box gave her a sense of security.

—Kristin L.

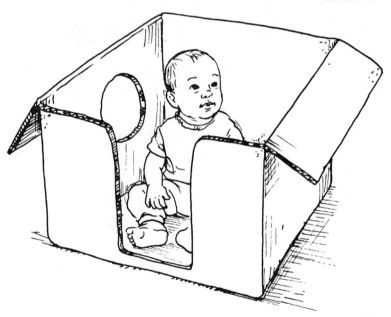

Chapter 17:
Toys and Playthings

242. Toys for Tots: Playthings for Your Baby

Toys are important for your baby's physical, cognitive, and social development. Try to find ones that are age appropriate.

Found playthings. Your baby will enjoy playing with a variety of household objects, but make sure they're safe. You might try cardboard boxes, pieces of paper, cloth, measuring spoons and cups, plastic containers and lids, an unbreakable mirror, gloves or mittens, a flashlight, and so on. Make sure to watch your child while he plays with the objects.

Store-bought. Most store-bought toys list the appropriate ages on the packages. Choose toys that fit your baby's developmental level.
Occasionally your baby may enjoy playing with something that's designed for older children; just make sure it's safe.

Open-ended. Some toys can be played with in lots of different ways. Babies continue to enjoy open-ended toys as they grow and develop. For example, a plastic cup and saucer can be banged, then used for a tea party, then turned into a spaceship. Toys that aren't open-ended tend to lose their attraction quickly.

Challenging. Offer your baby toys that challenge him to learn new skills. You don't want the toys to be so difficult that your baby becomes frustrated, but you don't want them to be so easy that he becomes bored. For example, younger babies are content chewing on nesting toys such as cups, rings, and blocks. As babies grow older, nesting toys offer additional challenges such as fitting them together.

Homemade. If you're creative and have the time, you can make your own baby toys out of simple household objects. For example, you can use worn-out socks to make puppets. Just make sure the toys are safe, durable, and appropriate for your baby's developmental level.

243. Quick Tip: Kids' Cupboard

I removed all the dangerous items from some of the lower cupboards in my kitchen, so my baby could explore them and play with what he found. He had a great time with the pots and pans and wooden spoons and plastic bowls. I made sure the other cupboards had childproof locks.

—Rena L.

244. First Plaything, Best Plaything: You!

You are the best plaything for your baby. You stimulate all her senses, which is how she learns.

Sight. Entertain your baby by dancing, bending, popping up, wiggling your tongue, opening and closing your mouth, widening and blinking your eyes, wrinkling your nose, shaking your head and hair, waving your hands, flapping your arms, jumping up and down, and so on.

Sound. Vary your voice in pitch and tone. Make other interesting sounds such as squealing, squawking, raspberries, blowing mouth bubbles, smacking your lips, clapping your hands, slapping your legs, singing silly songs, talking in funny voices, and so on.

Touch. Entertain your baby by letting her feel your clothes and body parts. Your skin is soft, your hair is fluffy or fuzzy or fine, your mouth and tongue are wet, your teeth are firm, and your clothes have a variety of textures.

Smell. You have a unique, familiar smell that makes your baby feel comfortable, secure, and safe. Entertain your baby by letting her smell your hair, clothes, hands, and so on.

Taste. You even taste good to your baby—and not just because she likes your breastmilk. Entertain your baby by letting her lick your skin, taste your fingers, suck your thumb, mouth your hair, and so on.

245. Watch It!: Toys for Babies Ages Birth to Three Months

From birth through age three months, your baby will enjoy a variety of toys, particularly ones that provide visual stimulation.

Mobile. Hang a brightly colored mobile above your baby's crib so she can look at it when she's awake. Try to find one that makes noises or plays a song.

Mirror. Hang an unbreakable mirror on the ceiling or wall near the crib or changing table, so your baby can see herself when she's lying down.

Music player. Play a variety of music including kids songs, classical music, and dance music. Don't turn the volume up too loud, though.

Lovey. Your baby will enjoy a variety of stuffed animals or other soft toys.

Squeaky toys. Squeezable, noisemaking toys are fun for your baby.

Noisy bracelets or anklets. Every time your baby shakes her leg or waves her arm, she'll hear the toy, which will help her learn about cause and effect.

Activity blanket. Your baby will have lots to do while lying on her blanket.

246. Mouth It!: Toys for Babies Ages Three to Six Months

From three to six months, your baby spends a lot of time exploring toys with his mouth to learn about size, texture, taste, weight, and other properties.

Rattle. Put a rattle in your baby's hand and let him wrap his fingers around it. He'll hold it for a few seconds, shake it, put it in his mouth, let it go, and eventually be able to hold it for longer periods of time.

Teething ring or bracelet. Although your baby isn't teething yet, he'll enjoy grasping a teething ring and bringing it to his mouth.

Plastic keys. Offer your baby lots of colorful, moveable toys that are easy to hold, shake, and mouth.

Small stuffed animals. Give your baby stuffed toys to hold and put in his mouth. The different textures will keep him entertained for a while.

Hands and feet. Babies love to play with their hands, fingers, feet, and toes.

Crib gym. Attach a crib gym to the side of your baby's crib so he can poke, pull, and play with the gadgets and gizmos.

Floor toys. Put your baby on his tummy and place toys nearby for him to grab.

247. Bang It!: Toys for Babies Ages Six to Nine Months

Between six and nine months your baby should enjoy holding, banging, dropping, and throwing toys—and having you retrieve them!

Drop toys. Good items to use for drop play are stuffed animals, pillows, beanbags, and other easy-to-grasp objects. Play Drop-and-Retrieve for as long as you can stand it; babies love it.

Banging toys. Get out your pots, pans, bowls, and wooden spoons and let your baby bang away. He'll also enjoy stacking, nesting, pouring, filling, dumping, "cooking," and sorting everything.

Balls. Give your baby a variety of balls of different sizes. He's learning to hold them, roll them, kick at them, and hit them. Try texture balls, rubber balls, musical balls, squeaky balls, and soft fuzzy balls. Have your baby sit propped up, and roll the ball toward him. Show him how to bat it, kick it, and roll it. Encourage him to chase a rolling ball, which gives him practice crawling.

Blocks. Your baby is beginning to learn the properties of blocks, aside from their taste and texture. He may start to stack them and knock them over. Show him how it's done. Start with large, soft blocks, then move to smaller wooden or plastic ones as your baby grows and develops.

248. Throw It!: Toys for Babies Ages Nine to Twelve Months

At this stage your baby begins to enjoy playing with older toys as they were designed, such as rocking and feeding a baby doll instead of chewing on it. She also loves dramatic play such as dressing up in hats and scarves. Provide plenty of cognitively stimulating toys such as those described below.

Fine-motor toys. Your baby's hands and fingers are becoming more skilled, so provide her with toys that enhance small motor movements, such as large-piece puzzles, small blocks, large wooden beads, sorting toys, playdough, and dolls. Watch her carefully so she doesn't put dangerous things in her mouth.

Gross-motor toys. At the same time, your baby is getting better at large-muscle movements. Provide her with gross-motor toys such as baby scooters, pushcarts, wagons, climbing toys, boxes (for tunnels), and household items for simple obstacle courses.

Carry toys. Your baby likes toys she can hold and carry while she practices walking, so give her small bags or handle toys to play with.

Push-pull toys. As your baby gets up on her feet, give her toys she can push and pull, such as toy strollers, toy grocery carts, wagons, and wheeled stuffed animals.

Make-believe toys. Toy telephones, steering wheels, cooking equipment, and other "real-life" toys allow your baby to begin acting out the things she experiences in her world.

Musical toys. Give your baby simple musical instruments such as toy pianos, harmonicas, and saxophones. Show her how to use the instruments so she can sing and dance and enjoy the rhythms and sounds.

Puppets. Use puppet fingerplays to entertain your baby and enhance her language skills. Classics include Pat-a-Cake, Peek-a-Boo, Itsy-Bitsy-Spider, This-Little-Piggy, Where-Is-Thumbkin?, Ring-around-the-Rosy, and Little Teapot.

249. Quick Tip: Play Party

After I had my baby, I called a few of the parents in my childbirth class and suggested we get together with our babies. We eventually formed a playgroup, which has been great for both the babies and the parents. Every week one of the parents hosts the playgroup. The babies get to spend time playing and learning how to share toys, and we chat about our latest parenting concerns.

—Jamaica J.

250. Toy Tough: Toy Safety

Not all toys are safe for your baby. Even though they may have been tested and approved by their manufacturers, playthings are constantly being recalled for safety issues. Here are some safety guidelines to follow before giving a particular toy to your baby.

Sharp edges. Are there any sharp edges or corners that could hurt your baby?

Choking hazard. Since your baby will inevitably put the toy in his mouth, make sure it can't fit through a toilet paper roll. If it can, then it's a choking hazard.

Small pieces. Are there any pieces that could come loose and become choking hazards?

Toxic materials. Is the toy covered with a safe material? Is it constructed of safe material? Make sure it hasn't been painted with lead paint and has no paint chipping off. You can buy lead tests at your local hardware store.

Durability. Is the toy going to stand up to your baby's vigorous play? Will it break apart if your baby bangs it, throws it, or chews on it?

Washable. Is the toy washable so you can keep it relatively clean for your baby?

251. More Tips on Toys and Play

Read. Your baby enjoys books from the time he's born, and perhaps even before. Listening to the rhythmic sound of your voice is soothing and comforting to your baby. Begin with paper-over-cardboard books or plastic books created specifically for young children. Also, read from picture books that feature lots of colorful illustrations, but keep them out of your baby's reach since they're easier to destroy.

Rotate toys. Let your baby play with a batch of toys for a few weeks, then put them away and bring out another batch. After a few weeks (or when he tires of the current batch), bring out a third batch. After he tires of those, bring back the first batch. They'll seem new because he hasn't played with them for a while, and also because he's more developed and may play with them differently.

Supervise. Monitor your baby during play time to make sure he doesn't get into dangerous situations.

Chapter 18:
Traveling with Baby

252. Baby Goes Bye-Bye: Traveling with Baby

Traveling with your baby doesn't have to be stressful. It can even be fun as long as you prepare. Allow plenty of time for packing and getting to your destination, so you can deal with unexpected disruptions. Make sure you keep your baby's diaper bag handy, and keep it filled with everything you're likely to need. (See page 80.) Take care of yourself by packing plenty of snacks and water, and take care of your baby by considering the following issues before and during your trip.

Health. Avoid traveling with your baby if she isn't feeling well.

Comfort. Your baby should be appropriately dressed for the weather. If you're flying, find out what the weather will be like at your destination.

Food. If possible, feed your baby before you go, and make sure she's been burped. Bring plenty of snacks and other food items, depending on what she's eating.

Rest. Make sure your baby gets a good nap before the trip, or make sure she's ready for a nap if you're going on a long drive, so she can sleep on the way. Take breaks every so often to break up the monotony.

Entertainment. Bring plenty of toys and stuffed animals to keep her entertained. Do fingerplays, sing songs, read books, play tapes or CDs of children's music, and so on.

253. Up and Away: Air Travel

If you're planning to travel by air, here are some tips to make the trip easier and more enjoyable.

Seating. Ask for bulkhead seating since that area tends to be roomier and more comfortable. You won't be able to stow your baby bag under a seat, however, since there won't be one in front of you. Just keep it handy in a nearby overhead compartment.

Assistance. If possible, have someone travel with you to help out with diaper changes and other situations. If you need to go to the bathroom, you'll have someone to hold your baby.

Takeoff. Make sure your baby sucks on something during takeoff and landing, to help normalize the pressure in her ears. Nurse her or give her a bottle or pacifier.

Diaper changing. Carry a changing pad to make diaper changes easier and more sanitary. Bring along plenty of diapers and wipes, since you never know when you're going to be stranded without luggage.

Extra outfits. Bring extra clothes for your baby AND you, in case your baby vomits or has a blowout BM.

Bottle warming. Ask the flight attendant to warm your baby's bottle, but be sure to test it before giving it to your baby.

254. Road Rules: Car Safety

Accidents are the number one cause of injury and death in children. About one-third of those accidents involve cars. Here are some tips for traveling safely with your baby.

Always wear your seat belt.

Always make sure your baby and other passengers are buckled in properly.

Always transport your baby in an age-appropriate, government-approved car seat. Make sure he's strapped in securely.

Always make sure car doors are locked and children can't open them without your permission.

Always check to see that fingers are out of doorways before closing doors.

Always make sure objects in your car are secure so they won't fly around and hurt your baby (or you) if your car needs to come to a sudden stop.

Always pay attention to the road. If your baby is upset and needs your attention, pull over first before tending to him.

Never hold your baby while riding in the car, and never place him in anything other than an approved car seat.

255. Sitting Safely: Car Seats

Car seats come in a variety of styles and safety features. Most hospitals require you to have a car seat for your baby when you leave the hospital. Double-check to make sure your baby's car seat meets current safety standards. Here are some tips for finding the best car seat for your baby.

Government approved. Make sure your car seat meets current federal motor vehicle safety standards. Make sure it fits your baby's age, weight, and height. Never substitute an infant seat for a car seat.

Installed properly. Read the instructions carefully, install the car seat properly, and make sure your baby is properly buckled in every time.

Safe location. The middle of the back seat is the safest location for the car seat. Never place your baby in the front seat.

Comfortable support. Make sure your baby's head is supported if he's too young to support it himself.

256. Quick Tip:
Car Seat Comfort

Whenever I put my baby in the car seat, he fussed. I finally realized that the car seat was either too cold or too warm, depending on the temperature in the car. So I pulled out one of his receiving blankets and placed it over the car seat to make it more comfortable. When he fell asleep in the car, I just picked him up in his blanket and transferred him to his crib. Throwing a blanket over the car seat also prevents the buckles from getting hot in the sun.

—Kelly V.

257. Quick Tip: Window Screen

Whenever I took my baby for a drive, I always worried that she would be bored and lonely in the back seat. So I put up pictures on the rear windows next to her car seat so she could have something interesting to look at. There are special pictures you can buy that don't impair the driver's visibility. I changed the pictures every few days to keep her entertained. They also shaded the sun quite nicely.

—Meredith B.

258. Quick Tip: Getting Out

My baby loved getting out of the house. He seemed to feel as cooped up as I did if we stayed in too much. I made a habit of getting out once a day, not just for errands, but for us. We'd take a walk to the park, go to the mall and window shop, go to a friend's house, visit animals at the zoo, do story time at the library, hang out at the baby gym, and so on. It was great for both of us.

—Bree S.

259. Quick Tip: In the Air

I had to take my baby on a cross-country flight, and I was worried about how he'd handle being in a plane for five hours. I found that walking him up and down the aisle really helped keep him entertained. He got a change of scenery and position, and he enjoyed looking at all the friendly passengers.

—Kelly V.

260. Quick Tip: Surprise Bag

I take a surprise bag with me whenever I go out with my baby. If she gets bored in the car or starts fussing at a restaurant, I get out a surprise to entertain her. I keep the surprise bag filled with special toys, stuffed animals, books, stickers, and so on. She gets to play with these special toys only when we're out on the town, so they never fail to keep her entertained.

—Barbara S.

261. Quick Tip: Out and About

I suggest taking your baby wherever you go right from the beginning. As he grows, he'll be used to going out in public and will easily adjust to new surroundings. We did this with our baby, and he really enjoyed being out and about. We never had to worry about taking him anywhere.

—Taya M.

262. Quick Tip: Set to Go

It used to take me an hour—at least—to prepare for running errands. I'd feed my baby, pack his stuff, change his diaper, then get myself ready. By the time I was finally ready to go, my baby would be hungry again! I eventually learned to restock the baby bag as soon as I got home, so it would be ready for the next trip. I also learned to get myself ready first before feeding and changing my baby. Organizing my time and keeping the baby bag filled helped me cut half an hour off the preparation time.

—Marie W.

263. Quick Tip: Grocery Store Fun

Most of the bigger grocery stores give out free slices of cheese, cookies, and other fun items. I always drop by those departments whenever I enter a store, to pick up a freebee to keep my daughter entertained while I shop.

—Susan W.

Chapter 19:
Keeping Baby Healthy

264. Rosy Cheeks: Keeping Baby Healthy

A healthy baby is a happy baby. One of your primary goals as a parent is to keep your baby happy by preventing illness and accidents as best you can. Being aware of your baby's normal behavior will allow you to notice clues when your baby may not be feeling well. Here are some tips for keeping your baby healthy.

Instincts. Parents often sense when their baby isn't feeling well, even if they don't know what's wrong. Because you spend so much time with your baby, you'll know when he's content and when he's distressed. Trust your instincts and call the doctor or nurse hotline if you feel something is wrong.

Crying. Tune in to your baby's cries and see if they sound different from his normal cries. A change may indicate a problem.

Expressions. Watch your baby's facial expressions, body language, and overall behavior for signs of a problem. If he's lethargic when he's normally active, something may be wrong.

Feeding. Pay attention to changes in your baby's feeding patterns. If he seems uninterested in nursing or bottle-feeding, he may have a health problem that needs attention.

Rash. Check your baby's skin for signs of a rash. A common diaper rash can cause considerable discomfort. Other rash-like symptoms may be caused by a bad reaction to medicine, food, or some other agent.

Germs. Some germs are dangerous to your baby and some are not. Be especially careful about spreading germs when changing your baby's diaper. Wash your hands thoroughly after changes or after handling toxic, dirty, or dangerous substances.

Exposure. Try not to expose your baby to sick children, especially those with colds or the flu. Germs are spread easily between children when they share food, toys, or physical contact.

Elimination. If your baby's elimination patterns change dramatically, such as considerably fewer wet diapers or symptoms of diarrhea or constipation, call your doctor or nurse hotline.

No smoking. Don't allow your baby to inhale second-hand smoke. Also, a smoker who handles your baby can transfer nicotine through your baby's skin, which can be harmful. Ask people to wash their hands before holding your baby.

Breathing. Avoid sprays, powders, perfumes, excessive dust, and other air pollutants that your baby may inhale. If he seems congested, call your doctor or nurse hotline and report the symptoms.

265. Doc Talk: Dealing with Your Doctor

Finding a doctor that fits your style is as important as finding a comfortable outfit that fits your body. Ask friends, relatives, and other health care providers for referrals, then set up interviews to ensure a good fit.

Questions. Ask the doctor about office hours, support hotlines, emergencies, health insurance and HMOs, hospital affiliation, breastfeeding, weaning, nutrition, treatment for common illnesses, immunizations, solid foods, and other issues you may be concerned about. If the answers seem reasonable and consistent with your parenting philosophy, you may have a good fit.

Problems. Don't be afraid to call your doctor or your clinic's triage service if you're concerned about something. You should be able to talk to a nurse immediately, and your doctor can call you back if he or she isn't available. Try not to abuse your doctor's time with minor problems you can solve yourself.

Phone numbers. Always have emergency numbers ready and visible near the phone. Important numbers include the doctor or nurse hotline, health clinic, hospital, poison control center, ambulance, fire, and pharmacy.

Preparation. Be prepared to describe your baby's condition in detail to your doctor or triage nurse. Take your baby's temperature and jot down her symptoms so you can give the doctor or nurse a complete picture.

266. Checking on Checkups: Visiting Your Baby's Doctor

Medical checkups are a regular part of your baby's overall health care. Checkups ensure that your baby's growth and development are on schedule.

Checkups. Your baby's first checkup occurs one to two weeks after birth. Your doctor will also want to do routine checkups at two months, four months, six months, nine months (optional), and twelve months.

Between checkups. Write down any questions or concerns you might have about your baby's health or development, so you can ask you doctor about them at your next visit. If you have urgent concerns, call your doctor immediately.

Family visits. If possible, both you and your partner should attend the checkups, so both of you can learn about your baby's health and development.

Entertainment. Bring something for your baby to play with, so she'll be entertained before and during the examination.

Full stomach. If possible, feed your baby before the doctor visit, so she'll be content and in a pleasant mood.

Happy face. Maintain a positive attitude about visiting the doctor, so your baby will sense your feelings and feel positive, too.

267. Checkup Checklist: What Happens at the Doctor's Office

Here are some issues you might discuss with your doctor during the office visit.

- Your baby's growth, including measurements of height, weight, and head circumference (You should receive information indicating your baby's growth rate compared to the average baby the same age.)
- Your baby's overall health and development
- Any signs of illness or disability
- Preventing health problems
- Feeding and weaning your baby
- Elimination patterns (urination and defecation habits)
- Encouraging healthy sleep habits
- Immunizations
- Periodic lab tests
- Questions you've written down ahead of time

268. Quick Tip: Doctor Visits

I was really intimidated by my doctor. I don't know why. Maybe because he always seemed so busy when I came to see him. I'd forget half my questions, and he always seemed to have his hand on the doorknob ready to leave. I started writing down my concerns before coming in, so I wouldn't forget them and so he'd be more encouraged to stick around. After all, he was my baby's doctor, and I was paying for his services. He finally accepted the fact that I was going to ask him questions and that I wasn't leaving until I was satisfied. It took me a while to assert myself, but I was glad I did.

—Devyn P.

269. Quick Tip: Bedside Manner

I found my first pediatrician through word of mouth. I'd been asking around, and the same name kept coming up. So I made an appointment and took my baby in for her first checkup. Well, he might have been a good doctor, but he had no bedside manner. I felt like I was bothering him with my questions. Plus, he kept us waiting for over an hour before each visit, no matter what time the appointment was. I finally changed pediatricians. It was hard quitting such a popular doctor, but I just wasn't happy. I found someone who was more my style. She really took her time and didn't make me feel like my questions were silly. I wish I had gone to her from the beginning.

—Deanna M.

270. It Won't Hurt a Bit: Immunizations

Clinics may vary in the exact preparation and scheduling of immunizations, so talk to your doctor. Here's a typical immunization schedule for the first year.

Birth. Hep B (Hepatitis B).

Two months. DtaP (Diphtheria, Tetanus, acellular Pertussis), IPV (Inactivated Polio Vaccine), Hib (Hemophilus influenza), PCV (Pneumococcal Conjugate Vaccine), Hep B (2–4 months).

Four months. DTap, IPV, Hib, PCV.

Six months. DTaP, Hib, PCV, IPV (6–18 months), Hep B (6–18 months).

One year. MMR (Measles, Mumps, Rubella; 12–15 months), Var (Varicella or chicken pox; 12–18 months), PCV (12–15 months), Hib (12–15 months).

271. Quick Tip: Make It Positive

I gave my baby a toy to hold before she got her shots. I also tried to keep a pleasant look on my face. I held her and soothed her and praised her (and tried not to overdo it). I hated those shots more than she did, believe me, but I tried to keep it positive.

—Rachel W.

272. Range of Reactions

Here are some of the reactions you might notice in your baby after she receives immunization shots.

Mild. Roughly fifty percent of babies have a mild reaction. Symptoms include swelling and soreness at the site of the injection, a low-grade fever (101°F), and irritability. Others symptoms may include a rash, diarrhea, and sleepiness. If your doctor approves, give your baby acetaminophen in a weight-appropriate dose. You may not need to call your doctor unless you're worried or the symptoms are increasing.

Moderate. Symptoms include those seen in a mild reaction, except there's a higher fever (102°F) and long-term crying. Give your baby acetaminophen and ice packs, and watch her closely. Stay in touch with your doctor or the nurse hotline, especially if the symptoms seem to worsen.

Severe. On rare occasions, a baby's temperature will climb to 105°F. The baby will cry nonstop, appear lethargic or sleepy, and may have convulsions. Call your doctor immediately.

273. Air Supply: Irregular Breathing

Newborn babies have to make an adjustment from liquid respiration in the uterus to breathing oxygen with their lungs after birth. This is a big change for a baby, and it takes time for the lungs to regulate themselves. Your baby may experience irregular breathing, short gasps, sighs, and pauses, all of which are normal. Some babies develop cold symptoms in the first few months (stuffy nose, raspy breathing, sneezing). This doesn't necessarily mean the baby has an infection. He might simply be clearing his air passages. Babies are nose breathers, which means they take in everything though their nasal passages, including dust, smog, and other things that can cause congestion. Here are some tips for reducing your baby's congestion.

Bulb syringe. Some doctors recommend a nasal bulb syringe or nasal aspirator for helping clear your baby's airway, especially before eating or sleeping. Other doctors don't recommend the bulb syringe because they believe babies will clear their air passages by themselves and shouldn't become dependant on assistance. Overaggressive, frequent suctioning can cause irritation. Give the syringe a try if your baby is very congested, but use it gently and sparingly.

Coughing. If your baby takes in too much milk, he may cough to clear his air passages. If this happens often, slow down his milk intake and give him more breaks during feeding.

Position and pat. Help your baby clear his congestion by laying him on his side or stomach and patting him gently to help settle the fluid. Never sleep him in this position, however. Holding him upright may also help drain the congestion. If necessary, try feeding him smaller amounts more frequently.

Caution: If your baby seems to have serious breathing problems, call your doctor immediately.

274. Quick Tip: Bathroom Air

My baby sometimes had trouble clearing her congestion when she had a cold, so I took her into the bathroom and turned on the shower. I kept the shower door open partway so the steamy air could easily escape into the room. Sometimes I put her in her infant seat while I took a shower. The moisture helped clear her nasal passages so she could breathe more easily.

—Connie P.

Chapter 20:
When Baby Is Sick

275. Sniff and Ah-Choo: When Baby Is Sick

In spite of everything parents and doctors do, babies still get sick. Here are some signs of illness and tips for what to do if your baby is ill.

Fever. Your baby's fever can be mild, moderate, or severe, depending on what the problem is. Most babies have a normal temperature of 98.6°F, although this varies from child to child. Anywhere between 97°F and 100°F can be considered normal. The most practical tools for taking your baby's temperature are rectal and axillary (underarm) thermometers. Rectal readings are usually about 1°F higher than axillary readings. Call your doctor if your baby has a rectal temperature of 100.4°F or higher.

Drowsiness. If your normally perky baby seems lethargic, sleepy, or unresponsive, she may be sick. Call the doctor if you think her drowsiness is caused by illness.

Pale or flushed skin. If your baby's skin changes from its normal color to a pale or flushed tone, this may be a sign that she's ill, has a fever, or is coming down with something. Call your doctor.

Loss of appetite. Babies' appetites ebb and flow, especially as they approach the end of the first year, so a decrease does not necessarily indicate illness. However, if you notice other signs of illness in conjunction with loss of appetite, such as fever or drowsiness, call your doctor.

Behavior. If your baby's behavior changes from what you'd consider normal, it could be a sign of illness.

Heartbeat. If your baby's heartbeat seems faster than normal, she may be sick. Normal heart rates for babies are 100–130 beats per minute when sleeping and 140–160 bpm when awake. Your baby's heart rate may be slightly higher if she's upset. Take her pulse and temperature and check with your doctor.

Breathing. If your baby's breathing seems fast, raspy, or especially congested, she may need to see a doctor.

Elimination. If your baby has a change in elimination pattern, check with your doctor.

276. Quick Tip: Mothers Know

One time I suspected my baby was sick, and I called the doctor. The nurse asked a bunch of questions and then told me it was nothing. But I had a strong feeling that my baby was sick. She just wasn't herself. I finally convinced the nurse that my baby needed to be seen by the doctor, and sure enough she had a serious ear infection. I strongly encourage parents to take their baby to the doctor if they think she's sick.

—Simonie W.

277. Home Remedies: How to Treat Minor Illnesses

Sleep. Let your baby sleep. Rest can do wonders for a baby who isn't feeling well.

Fluids. Give your baby plenty of fluids to help flush his system and prevent dehydration. Besides breastmilk or formula, offer your baby water, clear soups, and Popsicles.

Temperature. Make sure your baby is amply covered if he's chilled. If he's warm, don't overheat him by covering him even more. If he has a temperature of 100.4°F or higher, check with your doctor.

ABC. Here's a trick for treating diarrhea when your baby is old enough to eat solid foods. Offer him the ABCs—applesauce, bananas, and cereal. They're great for firming up loose stools. Don't overdo it, though, or you may end up with the opposite problem.

278. Quick Tip: Reference Book

I was worried about every little thing with my first baby. I was calling the doctor almost every other day. I finally bought a book that explains all the things about a baby's health. It really helped. I could look up the symptoms and figure out whether or not I should call the doctor. It calmed a lot of my fears and concerns, and it spared my doctor unnecessary calls.

—Connie P.

279. When Baby Has a Cough

A cough is usually accompanied by a cold or stuffy nose. Here are some tips for dealing with your baby's cough.

- If the cough keeps your baby awake or is accompanied by chills, fever, or vomiting, call your doctor.
- If the cough is accompanied by thick, yellow or green mucus, call your doctor.
- If the cough persists or gets worse, call your doctor.
- Treat your baby with cough medicine only after consulting your doctor.
- If the cough doesn't seem to be getting worse, if it doesn't seem to be interfering with his feeding and sleep, and if he doesn't have a fever, there's probably no cause for alarm. However, you should consult your doctor to make sure.

280. When Baby Has an Ear Infection

Ear infections are often accompanied by a cold, congestion, or teething.

- If your baby rubs her ear, doesn't seem to hear well, has drainage coming from her ear canal, is irritable, is in pain, or is crying excessively, call your doctor.
- Carry out your doctor's recommended treatment.
- Hold your baby upright while breastfeeding.
- If your baby has recurring ear infections, your doctor may recommend ear tubes to help with drainage or ventilation.

281. Quick Tip: Ear Tubes

My baby had chronic ear infections, and my doctor was becoming concerned that the chronic plugged ears would impair my baby's hearing and result in a language delay. My doctor referred us to an ear, nose, and throat specialist, who inserted tubes in my baby's ears to help drain the fluid. The surgery was scary for me, but my son didn't seem to mind. He was a lot less cranky without all those ear infections, and the tubes eventually fell out on their own.

—Rena L.

282. When Baby Is Vomiting

Most babies spit up occasionally, but your baby may also experience regular vomiting, projectile vomiting, or pyloric stenosis (an obstruction in the digestive system that causes milk and food to back up). Here are some tips for dealing with your baby's vomiting.

- If your baby has a distended (swollen) stomach, call your doctor.
- If your baby is crying nonstop, call your doctor.
- If your baby isn't gaining weight or is losing weight, call your doctor.
- Be prepared to give your doctor important details about your baby's vomiting, such as frequency, forcefulness, amount, and history.
- Watch for signs of dehydration including dry skin and lips, decreased wet diapers, listlessness, and sunken soft spot on head.
- If your baby is one-to-three months old and the vomiting is especially forceful, she may need to be evaluated for pyloric stenosis.
- After calling your doctor, give your baby a teaspoon of liquid every five minutes, offer her frozen pops made from oral electrolyte solutions, or breastfeed her.

283. When Baby Has Diarrhea

Your baby may develop diarrhea, which can be caused by gastrointestinal infections, colds, food allergies, and reactions to medicines. Here are some tips for dealing with your baby's diarrhea.

- If your baby's stools are explosive, watery, green, foul smelling, or blood-tinged, call your doctor.
- If your baby shows signs of weight loss or dehydration (page 299), call your doctor.
- Keep breastfeeding your baby.
- Offer your baby ABCs (applesauce, bananas, and rice cereal).
- Avoid juices. Instead, use one of the commercially prepared sugar and electrolyte solutions that help prevent dehydration.
- Call your doctor if the diarrhea continues.

284. When Baby Has Constipation

Babies' stools vary in consistency, frequency, and number, but you should take note of any significant changes in your baby's elimination patterns. Here are some facts and tips for dealing with your baby's constipation.

- Constipation may be caused by solid foods that can affect your baby's stools.
- Hard stools may become painful and cause your baby to fear elimination.
- If your baby experiences pain while passing stools or if he produces dry, hard stools, he may be constipated.
- Treat your baby by giving him laxative foods such as peaches, pears, and prunes, and by reducing constipating foods such as bananas and rice.
- Give your baby more water.
- Check with your doctor before using any pharmacy laxatives, enemas, or suppositories on your baby.

285. When Baby Has Allergies

Your baby may show signs of an allergic reaction, which could be caused by any number of things. Detecting the cause can be a challenge. Environmental allergies are fairly uncommon in the first year, but you may discover food allergies after introducing solids. Here are some tips for dealing with allergies.

- Signs of allergies include sneezing, coughing, wheezing, itching, runny nose, and frequent cold-like symptoms. Skin problems, such as eczema, may be associated with a food allergy.

- Possible causes of allergies include pollen, animal dander, mold, and food.

- Breastfeeding may help prevent the development of certain allergies.

- It's best to wait until six months before introducing solid foods, especially if your family has a history of allergies. Introduce one solid food at a time, and wait several days before introducing the next, to make sure your baby isn't allergic. Wait until the end of the first year before introducing cow's milk.

- Follow your doctor's recommendations on eliminating certain foods, changing formulas, or using skin remedies.

286. Giving Your Baby Medicine

Check with your doctor about how to give your baby medicine, when to give it, and how much. Here are some tips and guidelines to follow.

Read the label carefully. Follow the instructions exactly as they appear.

Check the dosage. Make sure you give your baby the right amount at the right time. Check with your doctor to see if you should awaken your baby to administer a dose of medicine.

Complete the dosage. Always give your baby the complete dosage of prescribed medication, and give it for the full length of time prescribed. Don't stop giving the medication because your baby seems to be better.

Side effects. Ask your doctor about possible side effects, so you know what to look for.

Other medications. Remind your doctor of other medications your baby may be taking at the time.

Caution: Always use child-resistant caps, and keep all medications out of children's reach.

287. A Spoonful of Medicine

It's not always easy to give medicine to a sick or squirmy baby. Here are some tips for making the task safer and easier.

- Disguise your baby's medicine in juice, milk, or mashed soft food.
- Try using a dosing spoon, dosing cup, or medicine dropper.
- Check to see if the medication should be given with or without meals (or liquids).
- Read the label to see if the medicine needs to be shaken before using or refrigerated after opening.

288. Quick Tip: Drop It

I had trouble giving my baby eye drops, so my pediatrician taught me the following technique. Wrap your squirmy baby in a blanket to keep her from wiggling around. Tilt her head back, gently lift one eyelid, then squeeze a drop in the corner of her eye. When she blinks, the medicine will spread to the rest of her eye.

—Holly K.

Chapter 21:
Keeping Baby Safe

289. Watch Out! Keeping Baby Safe

Accidents are the major cause of childhood death, so the best way to protect your child is to prevent accidents and injuries. Here are some facts to keep in mind and some tips for preventing accidents.

Mortality. A child has a 1 in 500 chance of dying from an accident before fifteen years of age.

Motor vehicle injuries. Most childhood injuries involve motor vehicles. Whenever you take your baby for a drive, buckle her safely in a car seat that's properly installed.

Common causes. Many childhood accidental deaths involve falling, drowning, choking, or poisoning. These are especially common among young children.

Injuries. A child has a 1 in 4 chance (each year) of experiencing an injury that requires medical attention.

Supervision. One of the major causes of accidents is lack of adult supervision. Many accidents can be prevented if parents watch their children closely. Always keep an eye on your baby, especially in environments that aren't childproofed.

Play space. Unsafe play areas are responsible for a high number of accidents, especially in crowded cities and rural areas with farm equipment nearby. Make sure your baby's play areas are safe, and check new environments for possible dangers.

Awareness. Parental failure to anticipate potential dangers is a major cause of childhood accidents. Children may swallow and choke on objects that have not been properly identified as choking hazards, they may climb and fall off of furniture that hasn't been perceived as dangerous, they may find ways to wrap things around their necks, and so on. If you're aware of potential problems, you're more likely to prevent injuries.

Activity level. As you might expect, very active children tend to have more injuries than cautious children. If your child is very active, you'll need to watch her even more carefully.

290. Quick Tip: Quick Kits

The first time my baby got a scratch, I looked all over for the Band-Aids. My older kids had gotten into them and taped them all over their bodies for fun! After that, I placed a bunch of ready-to-go first-aid kits all over the house, in the car, in the diaper bag, and even in my purse. I taped them closed with duct tape to keep the kids from getting into them. I found this really handy.

—Brooke S.

291. Preventing Potential Problems: Injury Control

Children will experience their fair share of scrapes and bruises, but serious injuries can often be prevented. Carefully assess the possible dangers in every situation your child finds himself in, and implement the following techniques for avoiding accidents.

- Never leave your crawling baby out of your sight, not even for a minute.
- Never leave your baby alone near water.
- Never leave your baby unsupervised with toys, other children, or pets.
- Take safety measures *before* your child develops the ability to put himself at risk for accident or injury.
- Teach your child about the dangers around him, without being overly frightening.
- Install smoke detectors on every floor in your home, and test them periodically.

Bonus tip: Don't overprotect your child, or he'll never learn to exercise caution. Keep him out of harm's way in the early months, but teach him how and why things can be dangerous as he starts crawling and walking.

292. Quick Tip: No-Fall Zone

I was told to be careful when putting my baby on a high surface or changing him on the changing table, because he might suddenly turn over and fall off. I finally figured out that the safest place (when you can't get to the crib) is the floor. A baby cannot fall off the floor. Just be careful if you have pets or older children.

—Ann P.

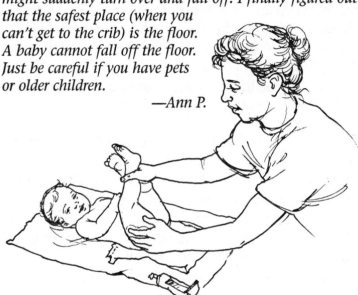

293. Childproof Your Home: The Bathroom

Childproofing your home is one of the most effective ways of preventing accidents and injuries. Your bathroom is loaded with potential dangers for your baby. Here are some tips for making sure your bathroom is safe.

- Put safety latches on all the cabinets.
- Make sure medicines, razor blades, cosmetics, cleaning supplies, and other dangerous items are locked away in latched cabinets.
- Turn your water heater down to 120°F to prevent accidental scalding.
- Place rubber mats in the tub to prevent slips and falls.
- Place a protective cover over the tub faucet to prevent your baby from bumping her head.
- Never leave your baby unattended in the bathtub. She can drown in less than an inch of water.
- Drain the water immediately after the bath.

- Keep electrical appliances, such as hair dryers and radios, unplugged and away from the water.
- Keep electrical outlets covered with safety caps.
- Keep the toilet seat down and latched.
- Never use glass containers in the bathroom. Always use rubber or plastic.
- Keep the bathroom door closed when not in use, and place a childproof doorknob cover over the handle.

294. Quick Tip: Catchalls

I bought several cheap plastic baskets and put one in every room in the house. Whenever I found stray toys or other items lying around, I'd just drop them in the nearest basket. At the end of the day, I'd carry each basket around and deliver each item to its proper place. It made cleaning up so much easier, and it helped preserve a safe environment for my baby.

—Rose L.

295. Childproof Your Home: The Kitchen

The kitchen is another room full of accidents waiting to happen. Here are some tips for childproofing the kitchen.

- Put safety latches on all cabinets and cupboards, except ones designated as safe play areas for your baby. Make sure your baby can't climb them, though.

- Install childproof locks on oven doors and stand-alone freezers.

- Remove all stove knobs when not in use.

- Make sure all cleaning supplies and other hazardous materials are locked up in cabinets or placed out of your baby's reach.

- While you're cooking, turn pot handles toward the back of the stove to prevent your baby from accidentally grabbing one and dumping the scalding contents on himself.

- Keep knives and other dangerous utensils locked up.

- Keep appliances unplugged when not in use.

- Make sure electrical cords are safely out of your baby's reach, and keep outlets covered with protective caps.
- Avoid tablecloths if your baby is able to pull himself to standing. He may yank on the tablecloth and bring table items down on his head.
- Make sure your baby is securely buckled into his highchair during mealtime.
- Keep fire extinguishers nearby.
- Don't hold your baby while cooking or cleaning.
- Keep matches out of reach or locked up.

296. Quick Tip: Highchair

Whenever I needed to do some cooking or cleaning in the kitchen, I put my baby in her highchair with some cooking utensils or other safe kitchen supplies. She especially loved the baster, wire whisk, and measuring cups and spoons. I was able to get things done and keep an eye on her at the same time.

—Barbara G.

297. Childproof Your Home: Baby's Bedroom

Be especially vigilant in your baby's bedroom, since she'll probably spend lots of time there.

- Check the crib for a Consumer Product Safety Commission label.
- The crib should be newer than 1978 and should not contain lead paint.
- Crib drop sides should be secure.
- Crib slats should be no more than 2⅜ inches apart, so your baby's head doesn't get caught between the slats.
- Make sure there are no splinters in the wood or cracks in the plastic.
- Make sure the crib does not contain any spires or knobs that your baby's clothes could get caught on.
- Check to see that the crib has no sharp edges or loose parts.
- Use a firm mattress to help prevent Sudden Infant Death Syndrome (SIDS).

- Remove crib bumpers, pillows, and other bed coverings that could cause your baby to get tangled up and smother.
- Make sure mobiles and crib toys are secure.
- Place the crib in a safe area away from windows and cords.
- Make sure you can hear your baby from every location in your home.
- Never tie toys to the crib slats. Your baby could strangle on the strings.
- Make sure your changing table pad has a security strap.
- Make sure all hazardous items, including diaper ointment and first-aid supplies, are out of your baby's reach.
- Secure large, climbable pieces of furniture (bookshelves, dressers, and cabinets) to the wall, to prevent your baby from tipping them over on herself.
- Secure floor lamps and other dangerous items that can be pulled over.
- Secure or hide all electrical cords, and make sure outlets are covered with childproof caps.
- Make sure all your baby's toys are safe and age appropriate.

298. Childproof Your Home: The Rest of the House

Don't relax yet. You still have the rest of the house to check.

- Pad sharp corners on tables, furniture, and fireplaces.
- Secure large, climbable furniture to the wall.
- Hide electrical cords and cover outlets with childproof caps.
- Place childproof doorknob covers on doors leading outside or into off-limits areas such as the basement.
- Keep guns and knives locked away. Guns should be stored unloaded with trigger locks engaged, and ammunition should be kept in a separate location.
- Make sure floors are free of small items that your baby could choke on.
- Remove plastic bags, balloons, sharp instruments, sewing gear, tools, cleaning supplies, and other potentially hazardous items.
- Tie up drapery cords so your baby can't strangle on them.
- Put stickers on sliding glass doors, and keep them locked.

- Remove poisonous plants so your baby can't swallow the leaves. Wrap netting around nonpoisonous plants so your baby can't get into the soil.
- Keep windows and doors securely locked, especially those that lead to the garage.
- Install safety locks on cupboards, cabinets, and drawers.
- Install safety gates near stairs and in front of fireplaces.
- Move expensive or otherwise valuable items out of your baby's reach.
- Make sure painted surfaces have been finished in lead-free paint.
- Locate fire exits, and practice a fire escape plan.
- Carefully clean up after parties.
- Make sure your garage door has a sensing device that prevents it from closing if something is in the way.

299. Surprise Attacks: Other Safety Issues

Here are some tips for dealing with other safety issues.

- Keep your purse out of your baby's reach.
- Make sure pacifiers are clean and safe. Never tie them around your baby's neck.
- Check strollers and playpens for safety.
- Watch hot coffee around your baby.
- Lock up alcohol, and do not allow illegal drugs around your baby.
- Don't let your baby have access to the garbage.
- When you visit another home, check for possible dangers and keep your baby in sight at all times. Carry pipe cleaners to function as temporary cabinet locks.
- Childproof your home and yard every few weeks. Your baby changes rapidly, and new hazards develop as she grows.
- Remind babysitters of the dangers to your baby, and go over a safety checklist with each sitter.

300. Quick Tip: Baby's Viewpoint

One of the best ways to check for hazards is to get down on the floor, crawl around, and see what your baby sees. Lie on your back and look underneath things, too. I found sharp nails poking out of the bottoms of end tables. You really need to get down into your baby's world to notice things you may not see otherwise.

—Ann P.

301. Watch Your Pennies: Choking Dangers

Choking is one of the main causes of death in children. Kids love to put things in their mouths—everything from bugs to dirt. Here are some common hazards.

- Popcorn, peanuts, and other nuts
- Grapes, cherries, and raisins that haven't been sliced to a safe size
- Chunks of apple or other hard fruits
- Chunks of hard, raw vegetables
- Peanut butter and other thick, sticky foods
- Hot dogs cut into circles or small chunks
- Small toys or parts of toys, coins, buttons
- Plastic bags, balloons

302. Quick Tip: Learn the Heimlich Maneuver

I really watched my baby, but somehow he got a hold of a peanut on the floor and put it in his mouth. He started to choke, and I turned him upside down and slapped him on the back. Luckily, the peanut came flying out. The whole thing freaked me out though, so I took a CPR class that focused on children's safety. I learned the Heimlich maneuver for babies, which is different from the adult technique, and I felt much more confident and reassured.

—Debbie B.

303. Quick Tip: Plastic Containers

I thought I was prepared to have my baby, but his room had so much gear, it was hard to keep it organized. So I went to the discount store and bought a bunch of plastic containers—buckets, stackable boxes, and plastic drawers. I labeled them "toys," "dirty clothes," "clean diapers," "blankets," "towels," and "miscellaneous." The containers allowed me to get everything off the floor, which made the room look cleaner and less cluttered. I later used the buckets to keep my son's toys organized, which made cleanup much easier.

—Sue W.

304. Quick Tip: Teach Safety

I followed all the childproofing guidelines before my baby started crawling, so I felt pretty secure about his safety. But I also believed in teaching him that certain things weren't safe. After all, you can't put everything out of your baby's reach. We worked on teaching him not to touch certain things, but we also let him gently handle things that weren't dangerous, such as the VCR. Giving him supervised access to things helped prevent them from becoming an obsession.

—Claire J.

305. In with the Good Air: Safe Indoor Air

Air pollution is typically thought of as an outside problem, but children can be exposed to many indoor air pollutants such as formaldehyde in carpets and building materials, carbon monoxide, radon, asbestos, cigarette smoke, paint fumes, lead, pesticides, and household chemicals. Studies have shown a link between these toxic substances and respiratory illnesses and other adverse health effects such as headaches, dizziness, fatigue, coughing, sinusitis, and nausea. Although it's difficult to avoid all air pollutants, you can be careful about what you have around your home that might increase the danger to your baby. Implementing preventive measures can help reduce the risks.

- Don't smoke, and don't let anyone smoke in your home.
- Increase ventilation by opening doors and windows daily.
- Replace toxic chemicals with environmentally safe products.
- Provide toys and art materials made of nontoxic substances.
- Check your home for dangers in building materials, such as asbestos and fiberglass.
- Make sure your heating and ventilating systems are clean and safe.
- Keep your home free of molds and dust by cleaning regularly.

306. Quick Tip: Chemical Change

My child has asthma, so I have to be especially careful to keep the house clean and free of dust and mold. I was trying really hard to keep things clean, but I didn't realize that some of my cleaning products were actually contributing to the problem. I got on the Internet and looked up some information on the U.S. Environmental Protection Agency website (www.epa.gov). It was a great help. They have all kinds of pamphlets and booklets that tell which products are harmful and which ones are safe. And it's all free. I got rid of most of my cleaning products and switched to nontoxic ones.

—Becky P.

307. Quick Tip: Safe in Bed

I thought I was so lucky to find an old crib at a garage sale for a very low price. It turned out the crib was so old, it had been painted with lead paint. The top coat of newer paint was peeling off, revealing the toxic lead paint underneath. Besides that, the crib slats were wider than 2⅜ inches, so my baby could get his head caught easily. If my mother's group hadn't warned me about these hazards, I wouldn't have known the dangers. Aside from clothing, which I still buy secondhand and wash thoroughly, I buy most of my baby's equipment new to make sure it's safe.

—Gail P.

308. Environmental Hazards: Lead

Lead poisoning is one of most serious environmental problems children face. Ingesting or inhaling lead paint chips or dust can cause brain damage, learning disabilities, and other health problems. Children who have elevated levels of lead in their system may not appear sick. The only way to find out is to have your doctor test your child's blood. Here are some common sources of lead contamination.

- Dust and paint chips from old, lead-based paint
- Recreational materials such as solders and fishing weights
- Older toys and cribs that were painted with lead-based paint
- Tap water coming through lead pipes
- Paint on the inside and outside of homes built before 1978
- Mini-blinds manufactured outside the United States before 1996
- Food stored in ceramic dishes, especially ones made outside the United States

309. Preventing Lead Exposure

- Test your home inside and outside for lead paint hazards, especially if it was built before 1978.

- Wash your baby's hands before she eats.

- Wash bottles, pacifiers, and toys often.

- Wash floors and windowsills to protect your baby from dust and peeling paint that might be contaminated with lead.

- Flush contaminants from lead pipes by running cold water for thirty seconds before using.

- Never use a crib made before 1978.

- Ask your local health department if there's a lead problem in your area.

- Before moving into a home or apartment, check with your realtor or landlord about possible lead contamination.

- Have your child tested for lead poisoning if you have any concerns about exposure to lead.

310. Environmental Hazards: Contaminated Drinking Water

Children drink a lot of water, usually much more than adults. Although water quality is protected by law in most areas, some water sources are not protected, such as certain private wells or surface water from lakes and rivers. A number of contaminants in drinking water can make children sick, including the following.

- Nitrates
- Chemicals
- Heavy metals
- Bacteria
- Viruses
- Radioactive particles

Many people use bottled water to avoid problems from tap or well water. However, you can't always be sure that bottled water has been properly purified. Bottled water is also more expensive and therefore not a reasonable option for many people.

You may consider using a water purification system. They're less expensive than bottled water (over the long term) and usually quite effective in removing contaminants. Most purifiers improve flavor as well.

311. Drinking Water: What You Can Do

- Determine your water source. If you're getting water from a municipal supply, contact your local water company for information about purity levels and possible contaminants.

- If you're using well water, make sure the water is tested every year and that your pump is in good working order. Make sure your well water is tested BEFORE you give it to your baby or use it to mix formula.

- If you're unsure about your water pipes, run the water for a few minutes before using it for drinking or cooking. Flushing the pipes will reduce the chance of contaminants getting into your water.

312. Quick Tip: Bottle Baby?

My husband and I got in the habit of drinking bottled water when we were in college, and we kept it going when we got married and had a baby. We avoided tap water because we were concerned about contaminants. But my daughter's pediatrician told us that bottled water didn't provide the fluoride necessary to protect my daughter's teeth. We needed to give her tap water so she would get the fluoride. I called the water company and learned that we were living in a very good water area. Now I make sure to give her tap water regularly.

—Kristin L.

313. Environmental Hazards: Carbon Monoxide

Carbon monoxide is a colorless, odorless, tasteless, toxic gas produced as a byproduct of combustion. Any fuel-burning appliance or other device has the potential to produce dangerous levels of carbon monoxide. Examples include furnaces, gas water heaters, fireplaces, wood stoves, gas stoves, gas dryers, charcoal grills, lawnmowers, snowblowers, and automobiles. If you have an appliance that isn't working properly, carbon monoxide may become trapped in your home.

Extended exposure to carbon monoxide can lead to brain damage and death. Approximately two hundred people are killed each year by accidental carbon monoxide poisoning, and an additional five thousand are injured. Watch for symptoms such as nausea, fatigue, and headaches, especially if several people in your home are experiencing the same problems. Here are some tips for preventing carbon monoxide poisoning.

- Install carbon monoxide detectors on every floor of your home, especially near sleeping areas.
- Have fuel-burning appliances and fireplaces inspected every year for carbon monoxide.

- Never sleep in rooms with unvented gas or kerosene space heaters.
- Don't use the oven to heat your home.
- Don't run automobiles or other gas-powered machines for long periods of time in an attached garage.
- Don't use charcoal grills in your home or in enclosed spaces.

314. Quick Tip: Carbon Monoxide Consciousness

I never knew carbon monoxide could pose such a threat in our home until I read about it in a newspaper article. When I realized our house was full of fuel-burning appliances— the furnace, gas heater, fireplace, and gas stove—I went out and bought a carbon monoxide detector to make sure everything was safe. Now I can sleep at night without worrying.
—Sue S.

315. Environmental Hazards: Mold

Children living in moldy environments are more likely to develop health problems such as allergies and asthma. Molds grow in moist areas like damp basements, shower stalls, bathtubs, wet carpeting, air conditioners, refrigerators, and so on. Here are some tips for preventing mold from becoming a problem in your home.

- Use dehumidifiers and exhaust fans to keep moist areas dry, especially bathrooms, basements, and the kitchen.

- Thoroughly dry any water-damaged materials, such as carpeting or wood floors, as quickly as possible. If effective drying isn't possible, replace or remove the materials.

- If your basement is susceptible to water leaking from floors or walls, take measures to fix the problem. Make sure the ground is built up around your home, and make sure the gutters are clean and properly installed so water can drain away from your home.

- Keep air conditioners and humidifiers clean and working properly.

- Wipe or squeegee tiles or shower doors after using the shower.

- Don't store firewood inside your home.

316. *Quick Tip: Old Moldy Home*

I kept my house pretty clean and never really worried much about mold. I thought it was something that showed up once in a while no matter what you did. Then my daughter started having respiratory problems. I took her to the pediatrician, who asked me about my house. How old was it? Was there a lot of moisture? How well ventilated was it? We happen to live in an old farmhouse, and I didn't realize how damp it was, especially under the house. We discovered a lot of mold, so we had an expert come in and help us clean it up. It took a lot of work, but my daughter's problems disappeared after we eliminated the mold.

—Simonie W.

317. *Quick Tip: Dangerous Plants*

I always keep the Poison Control number by the phone, in my purse, and in my baby's room. She once ate a leaf off a houseplant that I didn't know was poisonous. When I called Poison Control, they told me what to do, and she was fine. They also sent me a list of poisonous household plants. I got rid of all the plants in my house, just to be safe.

—Mia T.

318. Environmental Hazards: Chemical Pesticides

Pesticides are commonly used by farmers for protecting crops and by homeowners for maintaining lawns and gardens. Although chemical pesticides are designed to improve our quality of life by killing insects, weeds, and fungi, many of them are toxic to people and the environment. Last year over seventy-three thousand children were involved in pesticide-related poisonings. You need to be especially careful when your baby starts to crawl, since that's when she's more likely to get into trouble. Exposure to chemical pesticides and other chemicals can cause serious health problems. Here are some things you can do.

- Wash fruits and vegetables under running water before eating, and peel them whenever possible.

- Don't let your baby play in fields, orchards, or gardens where pesticides have been used.

- Buy fruits and vegetables that are in season, since they're less likely to have been heavily sprayed.

- Look for foods grown without chemical pesticides (organic foods). They may be slightly more expensive, but the added cost will be worth it.

- Avoid using chemical pesticides near your home. Instead, use alternative means of controlling weeds and bugs in your lawn and garden.

- Encourage neighbors to avoid using chemical pesticides, or ask them to notify you about what's being used and where.

- Never put pesticides or other chemicals in containers that children might mistake for food or drink.

- If you choose to use chemical pesticides, store them where children can't reach them, and keep them locked up.

319. Quick Tip: Pesky Pesticides

I hate to admit it, but when my back was turned, my son got into some pesticide products that were under the kitchen sink. Luckily I found him in time, but it scared me spitless. I babyproofed the whole house that day, removing all dangerous products and locking them up tight.

—Gay C.

320. Quick Tip: Litter Box Safety

I had a problem keeping my baby away from our cats' litter pans. They probably seemed liked sandboxes to him. I was worried about toxoplasmosis, a disease transmitted through cat feces, so I put a gate in the doorway to the laundry room, where we kept the litter pans out of his reach.

—Rena L.

321. Environmental Hazards: Sunburn

Your baby's skin is very delicate and susceptible to sunburn. Even on overcast days, thirty to sixty percent of the sun's ultraviolet rays can penetrate the cloud cover. Here are some tips for protecting your baby from sunburn.

- Babies under six months should not be exposed to direct sunlight. Keep them protected by hats, clothing, umbrellas, and other shading devices.

- For babies over six months, use sunscreen whenever exposing them to sunlight for more than a few minutes.

- First test the sunscreen on a small area of your baby's back to make sure it doesn't cause an allergic reaction. Make sure the sunscreen is broad spectrum with a sun protection factor (SPF) of 15 or higher.

- Minimize sun exposure during peak hours (10 AM to 4 PM).

322. Quick Tip: Fun in the Sun

I used to take my baby outdoors a lot. One day I noticed her arms getting pink really quickly, so I started carrying sunscreen and a sun hat in the diaper bag to protect her skin. I put the sunscreen on before dressing her, to give her initial protection; then I reapplied it to exposed areas every hour while we were outside. I also gave her little sunglasses. She didn't wear them much, but they were totally adorable.

—Patti C.

323. Environmental Hazards: Insect Repellents

New labeling requirements help ensure the safe use of insect repellents containing deet (diethyltoluamide). This active ingredient can be a health risk if not used as directed. It's important to apply deet safely, especially on children. Here are some tips for using insect repellents safely.

- Use an insect repellent designed specifically for children. Make sure it contains no more than ten percent deet.
- Don't apply the repellent near your baby's hands, face, or areas where his skin is scraped or irritated.
- Don't apply too much repellent. A light coating should do it.
- Don't spray repellent in enclosed areas or near food.
- Don't let your child breathe the repellent spray.
- Wash treated skin with soap and water after returning indoors.
- Wash treated clothing to remove the repellent.

- Don't let your baby handle products containing deet.
- Don't let your child play near stagnant pools of water where biting insects are more likely to be found.
- Don't dress your child in bright clothing or flowery prints in areas where biting insects are likely to be found.
- Don't use scented soaps, perfumes, or hair sprays on your child.
- If possible, apply the repellent to clothing rather than skin. This may be difficult when the weather is hot.
- If you notice your baby having an adverse reaction to the repellent, discontinue use, wash the skin, and call your doctor.

324. Quick Tip: Bug Bites

As a kid, I remember being lathered with insect spray whenever we were outside. My parents had no idea the lotion could be harmful. Now I check labels on repellents to make sure they're safe for my kids. Babies are especially sensitive, so I try not to use anything on my baby's skin unless it's absolutely necessary. And then I'm really cautious.

—Holly K.

325. Safeguarding Outdoor Play Areas

While outdoor play provides immeasurable opportunities for motor development and skill building, safety needs to be of prime concern. Here are some tips for creating a safe outdoor environment for your child.

- Fence in your yard (at least four feet high), and make sure the gate is latched. Avoid sharp wire or picket fences.
- Make sure climbing structures are sturdy, and place them on soft or grassy areas with lots of surrounding space.
- Check outside toys for broken parts, sharp edges, or hot surfaces.
- Make sure swimming pools are fenced in.

326. Quick Tip: Safe Snack?

My little boy loved playing outside. I always kept an eye on him, but he'd still take a tumble occasionally. Eventually I learned that the biggest threat was the dog bowl. He loved eating Lobo's food! The experts didn't warn me about that.
—Matt W.

327. Ticks and Lyme Disease: What to Watch For

Lyme disease has become the leading tick-borne illness in the United States. About fifteen thousand cases are reported each year to the Centers for Disease Control and Prevention. Lyme disease is caused by a bite from an infected deer tick. Here are some tips on how to protect your child from ticks and Lyme disease.

- Avoid low bushes and tall grasses in woodland areas.
- Use insect repellent in tick-infested areas. (See pages 336–337.)
- Ticks are most active between April and October, so be especially careful during that time.
- Dress your child in long sleeves and pants.
- Inspect your child for ticks after leaving high-risk areas.
- If you discover a tick, don't panic. Use tweezers to gently grasp the tick near its head, and carefully remove the whole tick without crushing it.
- An infected tick does not usually transmit the Lyme organism during the first twenty-four hours. However, if you're concerned about a tick bite, keep the tick in a plastic bag and bring it to your doctor.

328. Environmental Hazards: Radon

Radon is a radioactive gas that comes from the breakdown of uranium in rocks and soil. Radon can seep into a home through cracks in the walls and foundation. High levels of radon have been found in homes in many parts of the United States. Radon exposure does not cause symptoms right away, but long-term exposure can increase the risk of lung cancer. In fact, radon is believed to be the second most common cause of lung cancer (after smoking) in the United States. Here are some things you can do to protect your family.

- Check with your local health department about radon levels in your area.
- Test your home for radon by using a home test kit.
- Call the Radon Hotline (800-767-7236) for more information.

329. Quick Tip: Radon Raid

I had never even heard of radon until our neighbors told us their house had registered an unsafe level. We called the public health department, and they referred us to the official radon office for more information. They came right out and tested our house, and the results were even higher than our neighbor's! They told us what to do about it, including testing every so often with a home test kit.

—*Melanie E.*

330. Environmental Hazards: Asbestos

The presence of asbestos in your home is not usually a serious problem, as long as the asbestos materials don't become damaged and begin to release fibers. The best thing to do with asbestos that's in good condition is leave it alone! Disturbing it may create a health hazard where none existed before. If your house was built between 1930 and 1950, it may contain asbestos in the following areas.

- Roofing and siding shingles
- Textured paint and patching compounds used on wall and ceiling joints
- Artificial ashes in gas-fired fireplaces
- Walls and floors around woodburning stoves
- Vinyl floor tiles
- Hot water and steam pipes
- Oil and gas furnaces

331. Quick Tip: Asbestos Alert

I was well aware of the hazards when we started looking for a home. What I didn't realize was how hidden asbestos can be. We had a health inspector look at the property before we bought it, to make sure there were no hidden problems. Luckily he didn't find anything. But I never would have been comfortable until the place was checked.
—Chloe W.

332. Environmental Hazards: Electric and Magnetic Fields

Electric appliances, such as TVs, computers, and microwaves, produce electric and magnetic fields (EMFs) when they're turned on. Some scientists are concerned that EMFs may cause health problems such as cancer, although research has not yet established a definite link. Until more is learned about the possible hazardous effect of EMFs, you may want to reduce your baby's exposure by adopting the following safety measures.

- Keep your child at least three feet away from the TV when it's on.
- Move electrical appliances away from your child's bed, including baby monitors, radios, and clock radios.
- Keep your child away from microwaves when they're being used.
- Keep your child away from electric bedding such as waterbed heaters, electric blankets, electric mattress pads, and heating pads.

333. Environmental Hazards: Tobacco Smoke

Environmental tobacco smoke (ETS), also known as secondhand smoke, is the smoke breathed out by a smoker or the smoke produced from the end of a lit cigarette, cigar, or pipe. ETS contains many dangerous chemicals that have been proven to cause cancer. Exposure to ETS has been linked to three thousand lung cancer deaths each year—in people who don't smoke. Research also indicates that young children exposed to ETS have higher rates of lower respiratory illness, middle ear infections, and Sudden Infant Death Syndrome (SIDS). In addition, children with asthma who are exposed to ETS experience more severe symptoms and more frequent attacks. Here are some things you can do to prevent your baby's exposure to ETS.

- If you smoke, quit now.
- Don't let people smoke in your home, car, or anywhere around your baby.
- Make sure people who care for your baby do not smoke or allow smoke around your baby.
- Don't take your baby to places where smoking is permitted.

334. There Ought to Be a Law: Legislation

The government has introduced legislation over the years to reduce accidental deaths in children. Here are some of the most important changes and how you can ensure continued prevention of accidents.

Childproof caps have reduced poisoning deaths by eighty percent. Make sure childproof caps are securely attached on all medications, poisons, and other hazardous materials.

Flame-retardant sleepwear has reduced deaths from burning by ninety-seven percent. Make sure your baby's sleepwear is flame-retardant.

Fenced swimming pools and hot tubs have reduced drowning in children by fifty-one percent. Make sure your pool and hot tub are completely fenced in.

Car seats have reduced the number of deaths in children under the age of five by seventy percent. Always buckle your child in a car seat that's properly installed.

335. The 411 on 911: Emergency Information

Keep emergency information handy so you can locate it quickly when you're under stress. This information will also be helpful to babysitters. Discuss with your doctor ahead of time the best way to handle an emergency. Here are a few things to keep near the phone.

- Important personal phone numbers including home, work, cell phone, grandparents, friends, close neighbors, and others
- Emergency phone numbers including the doctor, hospital, clinic, specialists, pharmacy, ambulance, fire department, and local poison control center
- Your baby's medical conditions or allergies
- Medicines your baby may be taking

336. Quick Tip: Instant Info

I made several copies of my baby's emergency information and kept them all around the house for quick and easy access. I also gave them to neighbors and relatives, and carried them in my purse and car. I always had one available for my babysitters, too.

—Barbara S.

Chapter 22:
Beginning Discipline

337. "What Part of No...?": Beginning Discipline

Discipline means different things to different people. Some consider it "punishment"; others understand it to mean "guidance" or "teaching," as in "disciple" or "follower." Most child developmentalists today are stressing a nonviolent approach to discipline. They're encouraging parents to move away from punishment toward a teaching model of discipline.

When to begin. The foundation for effective discipline begins at birth. The relationship you form with your baby will help you guide her behavior later on.

Attachment. A close attachment helps you sense what your baby needs before it becomes a concern. Your baby learns to trust you, which is an important aspect of positive discipline.

Win-win. Every "teachable moment" should be a win-win situation for babies and parents. Your baby will feel safe and secure because she needs you to establish boundaries of behavior, and you feel good because you don't have to resort to shouting, threatening, or hitting your child.

Prevention. Avoid unnecessary power struggles by preventing confrontations from developing. For example, remove dangerous objects from your baby's play area, so you don't have to say, "No, don't touch," all the time.

Age-appropriate behavior. If you understand your baby's development, you'll realize that certain behaviors are normal at certain ages. For example, knowing that your six-month-old will put things in her mouth to learn about them will encourage you to remove choking hazards and thereby avoid unnecessary confrontations.

Offer learning opportunities. Don't set your baby up for failure. Give her opportunities to behave positively rather than negatively. For example, give her challenging toys to master rather than scolding her for getting into your purse when it shouldn't be within her reach.

Personality. Understanding your baby's temperament, emotions, and energy levels throughout the day will help you guide her behavior. If she's sick, she'll likely behave differently than if she's feeling fine, so be sensitive to changes in her routine that might influence her behavior.

Problem-solve. Remember that all behavior is motivated. Try to determine the cause of your baby's behavior so you can eliminate problems that might be influencing it. For example, if she's irritable and uncooperative, she may be teething. Check for other signs and administer appropriate remedies.

Bonus tip: Babies don't deliberately manipulate their parents. Your baby uses trial and error to learn how to interact with you, so it's up to you to practice positive discipline. That way your baby will learn appropriate behavior without being fearful of shouting or spanking.

338. Parenting Plans: Childrearing Choices

There are many different parenting styles defined by a variety of child development experts. Here are the three basic types.

Authoritarian. Authoritarian parents believe their word is law and children should respect authority. Discipline is strict and usually involves spanking or at least the threat of it. Many child developmentalists argue that children of authoritarian parents tend to be unhappy, at risk for committing violent behavior later on, and less motivated academically.

Permissive. Permissive parents don't seem to care what their children do. Discipline is lax. Children of permissive parents tend to be confused, undisciplined, and insecure, and they tend to have lower academic skills.

Authoritative/democratic. Authoritative/democratic parents generally listen to their children and try to understand their viewpoint. They prefer nonviolent forms of discipline, and tend to stress teaching over punishment. They compromise with their children when it's appropriate, but they always have the last word based on what's best for their children. Both parents and children win. Children of authoritative/democratic parents tend to be happy, independent, socially competent, and academically successful.

339. Quick Tip: Like My Parents

My father was really strict and my mother was really lenient, so I learned to play them according to what I needed. But it drove me crazy because I never knew which parent would win and what I'd be allowed to do. After becoming a parent myself, I decided to be somewhere in between. I set clear boundaries, but I also listened to my kids and let them have some say in the decisions. I think this taught them a sense of responsibility. I tried to be consistent, like the books say, but some days were better than others, depending on how tired I was. I always tried to do the best I could.

—Donna B.

340. Read the Rules: Limits and Boundaries

Discuss your parenting styles with your partner and talk about what you ultimately want for your child and yourselves. Effective communication will help you make solid decisions regarding discipline techniques, setting limits, and principles of behavior. Here are some basic guidelines for setting limits for your child.

Respect others. Teach your child to cause no deliberate harm to other people. It's important that she learns to respect others.

Respect himself. Teach your child to cause no deliberate harm to herself. She should learn to respect herself as much as she respects others.

Respect property. Teach your child to cause no deliberate harm to property. She should learn to respect both her own and others' things.

341. Quick Tip: No-Share Zone

My baby had trouble sharing his toys. So instead of making him share all his toys when a friend came over, I let him pick out some special toys that he didn't have to share. We put those away while the friend was over, and took them out again when the friend was gone. In the meantime, my baby shared everything else without a problem.

—Kristin L.

342. Say No to No!

No is a powerful word that shouldn't be overused.

Spare the word. Save *no* for times when you really need it, such as when your baby is endangering herself or doing something you really don't want her to do. Childproofing your home can minimize situations in which you'd be tempted to overuse *no*.

Explain why not. Get in the habit of explaining in simple terms why you don't want your baby to do something. Use phrases like "Danger, danger," or "That can hurt you." She'll eventually be able to understand your meaning, and your respectful tone will create a climate of mutual trust. Most importantly, you'll be teaching her the real reason why she should avoid something, instead of annoying her with, "Because I said so!"

Look serious. When you say, "No," look like you mean it. Use a firm voice and a serious expression. You don't have to scream.

Respect your baby. Whenever possible, provide your baby with opportunities to exert control over her environment. She needs your boundaries to feel safe, but she also needs to develop her sense of self. Letting her make choices will actually result in her being more compliant when you really need it.

343. Create a Safe Environment

Set up your home so it's both stimulating and safe for your baby to explore. Take the time while your baby is still young, so you can avoid unnecessary confrontations down the road. Your baby will be free to play, and you won't waste a lot of time restricting his behavior.

Limit access. Put up gates in front of stairs, and close doors to prevent access to off-limits areas.

Store stuff.
Put dangerous or breakable items out of your baby's reach, so he isn't tempted to play with them, causing an unnecessary confrontation.

Childproof. Go over every room in your home (even areas that will be off limits) to make sure each one is safe.

Provide fun. Set out lots of fun things for your baby to play with, so he won't be inclined toward mischief. In addition to his regular toys, give him access to pots, pans, and other safe household items. If possible, designate a special cabinet or shelf where he can keep his things.

Keep watch. Even though the environment should do most of the work, never leave your baby unattended. Babies have a knack for finding trouble even when parents think they've eliminated the options.

344. Quick Tip: Drive Them to Distraction

I found the best way to deal with potential problems was redirecting my baby's attention. If he wanted to play with something that was off limits, I'd distract him with another toy by making it look more fun. If he wanted to go into the bathroom to explore, I'd bring him into the living room where there were lots of toys to keep him occupied. The store was the worst—he wanted everything he saw. I'd give him a small bag of potato chips to keep him entertained. The puffy bag made a great crinkly noise.

—Bree S.

345. Spank-Free Zone

Many developmentalists now consider spanking too harsh a punishment for a baby or child. Here's why.

Spanking is frightening. Imagine a towering giant reaching down and striking you! That's how a child feels when being hit by a parent. Don't scare your child into submission.

Spanking is temporary. Striking your child only temporarily halts the negative behavior. Spanking may also produce more negative behavior in the long run, as children learn to use violence to get what they want.

Spanking is unhealthy. Spanking breeds resentment and anger, which a child may suppress in front of parents but release in other ways such as hitting a younger sibling.

Spanking is abusive. We've now learned that spanking can lead to child abuse. Striking your child in anger is easy to do when you become enraged at misbehavior. However, because spanking is ultimately ineffective, you may feel the need to resort to more frequent and more violent spanking. Don't start, or you may not be able to stop.

Spanking is not educational. When you hit your child, you only teach her fear. Instead of learning to avoid the behavior because it's wrong, a child learns to avoid the behavior because she'll be spanked.

Spanking is hypocritical. It's hypocritical to hit your child for hitting. Instead, model the behavior you want her to imitate.

346. Quick Tip: Offer Choices

When my baby finally learned to say, "No!" he said it all the time. I knew it was important for him to make decisions once in a while, so I started giving him choices that did not include no as an option. For example, instead of saying, "Do you want juice?" I'd say, "Do you want juice or milk?" It worked really well.

—Connie P.

347. Quick Tip: No Hitting

I thought it was really weird telling a child not to hit, then spanking him for hitting. I was spanked as a child, and all it did was make me more devious and angry. I swore I'd never spank my kids. It doesn't teach anything but fear. Instead, I talk to them, give them breaks, redirect their attention, and try to make the punishment fit the crime. I want growing up to be a learning experience for them, not a power struggle. I can't imagine slapping my baby or any child for any reason whatsoever.

—Kelly S.

348. Catch Them Being Good: Using Positive Reinforcement

Parents tend to notice their child when he's getting into mischief, but often don't notice when he's doing something good. One of the best ways to guide your child's behavior is to praise him when he's doing the right thing.

Catch him being good. If your child is having a problem with shouting in the house, don't wait for him to start screaming before you act. Instead, say, "You're using a nice quiet voice today!"

Give your child lots of praise. When your baby does something good, praise him in a way that's related to his behavior. Instead of saying, "Good girl," say, "You're doing a great job eating with your spoon!"

Avoid criticism. Instead of criticizing unwanted behavior, promote an acceptable alternative. For example, say, "Tap softly," instead of, "Stop pounding!"

Stay close. By staying nearby and watching your baby closely, you can redirect his behavior before he gets into trouble. If he's about to put a toy in the VCR, show him a different place to put it.

349. Quick Tip: Tantrum Trick

My baby started having temper tantrums around age one. He'd throw himself on the floor, kick, scream, and cry until he almost turned blue. I didn't know what to do. Finally I thought, "What would I want if I were having a tantrum?" I'd want someone to comfort me. So that's what I did. I picked him up and held him tight and let him cry. Then I began talking to him in a soothing voice. Eventually he calmed down. I'm not sure if he knew why he was so upset, but human contact seemed to be the cure. Sometimes we just need to be held.

—Brooke S.

Chapter 23:
Returning to Work

350. Mommy's Going Bye-Bye: Returning to Work

Returning to work is a major concern for many parents, especially mothers who have mixed feelings about leaving their babies. Most child developmentalists recommend that one parent stay home for the first year of a baby's life. Unfortunately, that's not possible for many parents, mainly because of financial pressures. About twenty-five percent of mothers with babies under one year of age work outside the home, and about ninety percent of fathers work outside the home. Here are some important questions to ask before making your decision.

- Do you enjoy your job?
- Does it provide a good income?
- Is it rewarding?
- Why do you want to continue working?
- What are the benefits of staying home?

- How much would child care cost, compared to the income from your job?
- Do you want to return to work?
- Do you really have to return to work?
- Can you work part-time?
- How long can you stay home without losing your job?
- Who do you want raising your child?

351. Quick Tip: Pump It

When I went back to work, I wanted my baby to continue having breastmilk, but I wasn't very good at expressing the milk. I barely got a few teaspoons after really working at it. My friend recommended a breast pump that worked well, although it was tricky at first. It looked like a bicycle horn, and I had to learn to take it slow or it would really hurt. I got enough milk to fill a bottle (the pump even had a bottle attachment), and I'd freeze it until it was time for the day care provider to give it to my baby.

—Bonny J.

352. Home Sweet Home: Benefits of Staying Home

- You'll be there to respond to your baby's needs.
- You'll be able to witness your baby's subtle developmental changes.
- Your attachment process will be uninterrupted.
- You'll be available for the teachable moments.
- You'll save money on child care.

353. Quick Tip: No More Work

I had planned to go back to work a few weeks after having my baby. I had everything lined up and had told my boss I'd definitely be back. But the moment I saw my baby, I didn't want to leave him! After several sleepless nights, I did some calculating and figured if we cut down on luxuries, we could manage. The day before I was supposed to return to work I called my boss and told him I wasn't coming back. He was surprisingly understanding. Maybe he'd been through this before. It was such a relief to me, and I've never regretted it. I started doing some typing at home to make a little money. Maybe staying home isn't right for everyone, but it's right for me.

—Julie L.

354. The Same Four Walls: Problems with Staying Home

- You may get bored.
- You may feel isolated, unchallenged, understimulated, and alone.
- You may feel overwhelmed and without support.
- You may resent your baby or partner for interfering with your career.
- You may get burned out from doing child-care duties all day.
- You may be criticized by people who see you as lazy and unmotivated.

355. Quick Tip: Going Nuts

My mother stayed home with us, so I planned to stay home with my kids. But after a few weeks at home with my baby, I was stir-crazy. I missed seeing my coworkers and getting out of the house, and I missed the extra money. But I didn't want to leave my baby with a sitter, so I decided to try day care. It worked out great. My baby had friends to play with, and I felt competent and useful again. And the money didn't hurt either.

—Mary Fran K.

356. Paycheck Payoffs: Benefits of Working

- Your baby will learn to bond with other people.
- You'll probably make more than enough money to cover child-care costs.
- You'll enjoy the intellectual stimulation of your job.
- You'll enjoy the company of your coworkers.
- Your baby will likely spend time with other babies his age.
- Coming home to see your baby will be very exciting.

357. Working Worries: Problems with Working

- You may miss your baby so much you won't be able to concentrate on your work.
- You may feel guilty about leaving your baby.
- You may feel sad or disappointed when you miss your baby's milestones.
- You may feel overloaded working full-time (or even part-time) and caring for your baby and your home.
- You may be overly tired and cranky when you get home.
- You may feel you need to spend every moment with your baby when you're not at work, to make up for lost time.
- You may be criticized for being selfish and neglectful of your baby.

358. Career Compromises: What Are Your Choices?

So what's a parent to do? Work? Stay home? Or do both? Here are some tips to help you make a decision.

- Extend your maternity or paternity leave for as long as possible, and ask your partner to do the same. The Family and Medical Leave Act requires your employer to give you up to twelve weeks of unpaid leave after the birth of your baby, unless your company has fewer than fifty employees.

- Evaluate your priorities and figure out what's more important to you—working or staying home.

- Be realistic about your financial needs, and be honest about the reality of getting by on less money. It can be much tougher than you think.

- Be creative about making money in other ways, such as expanding a hobby and turning it into a money-maker.

- Work part-time if possible, or job-share with another parent who's in the same position as you.

- Ask your employer about working flexible hours or working from home.

- Enjoy your time with your baby when you're home, rather than feeling guilty about leaving him.
- Take your baby to work with you, if possible.
- Explore on-site child care or investigate the possibility of starting a child-care facility at your place of employment.
- Consider starting a day care at your home.
- Juggle work hours with your partner.

359. Quick Tip: Ease Off Feeding

When I went back to work, I tried to stop breastfeeding all at once, but my breasts got really engorged. So I fed my baby in the morning and again at night, and slowly but surely my breasts became less sore. I eventually eliminated the morning feeding. After a few more weeks, I stopped the night feeding, too. Quitting gradually instead of cold turkey was much easier on both of us. I wish someone had told me this earlier, before I tried it the hard way.

—Sue W.

360. Who's Minding The Baby?: Choosing Child Care

If you decide to go back to work, you'll need to find quality child care. Consider the following options.

- Partner
- Nearby relative
- Home day care provider
- Commercial day care center
- On-site day care
- Babysitter
- Nanny or au pair
- Parent co-op

361. Quick Tip: Not Guilty

I'd like to be home with my baby, but we need my income to help pay the mortgage and provide the basics. Plus, I love my job. I'd spent years going to school to become an attorney, and I got pregnant right after I got my first job in a law office. I miss my baby during the day, but I'm so excited to see him when I get home. I have a great nanny who comes to my home and takes excellent care of my baby. I may quit working in a few years, but right now my baby seems happy, and I feel good about realizing my career goal.

—Jackie S.

362. Kid Country: Choosing a Child-Care Center

Here are some questions you should ask when researching a child-care center.

- Does the facility have a state license?
- What are the teachers' credentials?
- What's the center's philosophy?
- How do they handle a sick child?
- How do they handle a crying child?
- Is the site safe, clean, and attractive?
- Is there plenty of space and safe equipment for the children?
- What's the ratio of caregivers to children? (There shouldn't be more than four babies to each adult.)
- Does the staff enjoy working there?

363. The Match Game: Finding the Right At-Home Caregiver

Here are some tips for finding a good at-home caregiver.

- Ask friends and neighbors for referrals.
- Contact local agencies for lists of day care providers in your area.
- Interview several candidates before deciding.
- Ask questions about things that matter to you, such as nurturing techniques, naps, food, discipline, number of kids in the day care, and so on.
- Trust your gut; take your feelings into account before making a final decision.
- Get references and check them out.
- Check with your local city, county, or state agencies to see if there have been any negative reports about the caregiver.

364. Quick Tip: Surprise Visit

When I finally found the day care provider that seemed best for my child, I decided to make sure by dropping by unannounced one day. I wanted to see if the environment was safe, if the atmosphere was calm and positive, and if the caregiver was really sensitive to the kids. I was delighted by what I found. I made a point of dropping by from time to time, and I always found it pleasant. I recommend this to all parents who have children in day care. Most good providers welcome random inspections.

—Joanne M.

365. Question the Candidates: What to Ask At-Home Caregivers

Here are some questions to ask at-home caregivers.

- How will you handle my baby if she cries?
- How will you comfort my baby if she's upset?
- How much will you hold my baby throughout the day?
- What kind of activities will you provide for my baby?
- Will you talk to my baby?
- How will you handle feeding my baby?
- How will you discipline my child?
- Do you have any questions about my baby?
- What's your philosophy about raising children?
- Do you know the basic developmental milestones for babies?
- What kind of safety precautions have you taken at the site?
- Are you in good physical condition?
- Do you smoke?
- Do you have the TV on during the day? What programs do you watch?
- How do you handle your household chores when you're watching the kids?
- Why did you get into child care?
- Do you have a child-care license?
- Is there anything you'd like to ask me?

Appendix I:
Where to Find Help

Adoption Resources
www.adopting.org; www.adop-tion.org
Information on adoption

American Academy of Allergy,
Asthma, and Immunology
414-272-6071
www.aaaai.org
Information on allergies and
asthma

American Academy of Pediatrics
800-433-9016
www.aap.org
Information on children's health
and development

American Association for Home-
Based Early Interventionists
800-396-6144
www.aahbei.org
Information for parents who
have young children with disabilities

American Foundation for the
Blind
800-AFBLIND
www.afb.org
Information on blindness

American SIDS Institute
800-477-SIDS
www.sids.org
Information on Sudden Infant
Death Syndrome

Association for Children with
Down Syndrome
516-933-4700
www.acds.org
Information on Down Syndrome

Babies Today
www.babiestoday.com
Information on baby care

Baby Daily Calendar
www.babydaily.com
Information on baby's milestones

Baby Place
www.baby-place.com
Information on a variety of baby
topics

Blue Suit Moms
www.bluesuitmom.com
Information for the working
mother

Breastfeeding
www.breastfeed.com;
www.breastfeeding.com
Information on breastfeeding

Car Seat Safety
866-SEATCHECK
www.seatcheck.org
Information on car seat safety

Child Care Aware
800-424-2246
www.childcareaware.org
Information on improving child
care

Children's Health
www.kidshealth.org
Medical information on children's health issues

Cleft Talk
800-242-5338
Information on cleft palates

Club Mom
www.clubmom.com
Information and support for mothers

Consumer Product Safety
Commission
800-638-CPSC
www.cpsc.gov
Information on product safety

Cystic Fibrosis Foundation
800-FIGHTCF
www.cff.org
Information about cystic fibrosis

Dads Today
www.dadstoday.com
Information and support for fathers

Depression after Delivery
800-944-4773
www.depressionafterdelivery.com
Information on dealing with postpartum depression

Dr. Spock
www.drspock.com
Information on parenting

Dr. Toy
www.drtoy.com
Information on toys and educational playthings

Family Fun
www.family-go.com;
www.childfun.com
Tips for creating family fun

Federation for Children with
Special Needs
617-236-7210
www.fcsn.org
Information on children with special needs

Fisher-Price
www.fisher-price.com
Information on activities, playgroups, and toys

Food Allergy Network
www.foodallergy.org
Information on food allergy awareness

Idea Box
www.theideabox.com
Information on early childhood education and activities

International Association of
Infant Massage
800-248-5432
www.iaim-us.com

La Leche League
800-LALECHE
www.lalecheleague.org
Information on breastfeeding

March of Dimes Birth Defects
Foundation
888-663-4637
www.modimes.org
Information on birth defects

National Association for Family
Child Care
800-359-3817
www.nafcc.org
Information on child care

National Center for Fathering
913-384-4661
www.fathers.com
Information for fathers

National Child Care Information
Center
800-616-2242
www.nccic.org
Information on the child care
delivery system

Prevent Child Abuse America
800-CHILDREN
www.preventchildabuse.org
Information on child abuse
prevention

National Down Syndrome
Society
800-221-4602
www.ndss.org
Information on Down Syndrome

National Easter Seal Society
800-221-6827
www.easter-seals.org
Information, support, and services to children and adults with
disabilities

National Highway Traffic Safety
Administration
888-327-4236
www.nhtsa.dot.gov
Information on car seat safety

National Information Center for
Children and Youth with
Disabilities
800-695-0285
www.nichcy.org
Information on disabilities

National Institute of Child
Health and Human
Development
800-370-2943
www.nichd.nih.gov
Information on maintaining the
health of children, adults, families, and populations

National Organization of
Mothers of Twins Clubs, Inc.
www.nomotc.org
Information on parenting twins
and multiples

National Organization of Single
Mothers
www.singlemothers.org
Information to help single
mothers

Parents Educating Parents and
Professionals for All Children
www.peppac.org
Information and support for
parents of children with
disabilities

National Safe Kids Campaign
202-662-0600
www.safekids.org
Up-to-date safety information
for parents and child-care
providers

National Safety Council
800-621-7619
www.nsc.org
Information on child safety

Parents Anonymous
909-621-6184
www.Parentsanonymous-
natl.com
Information on child abuse
prevention

Parents of Premature Babies
www.preemie-l.org
Information and support for
parents of premature babies

Parenting
www.iparenting.com;
www.parenthoodweb.com
Information for parents regarding
children

Postpartum Education for Parents
www.sbpep.org;
www.postpartumstress.com
Information on postpartum
emotions

Sickle Cell Disease Association of
America
800-421-8453
www.sicklecelldisease.org
Information on sickle cell anemia

SIDS Alliance
800-221-SIDS
www.sidsalliance.org
Information on Sudden Infant
Death Syndrome

Spina Bifida Association of
America
800-621-3141
www.sbaa.org
Information on spina bifida

Stay-at-Home Dads
850-434-2626
www.slowlane.com
Information and support for
stay-at-home dads

Stepfamily Association of
America
www.stepfam.org
Support and advice for families
raising children from previous
marriages

Toddlers Today
www.toddlerstoday.com
Information on raising your
toddler

Twin Stuff
www.twinstuff.com
Information on twins and
multiples

United Cerebral Palsy
Association
800-872-5827
www.ucp.org
Information on cerebral palsy

Appendix II:
Books on Babies and Parenting

The Baby Book: Everything You Need to Know about Your Baby from Birth to Age Two
William Sears, Martha Sears, Little Brown & Co., 1993

Baby Play and Learn
Penny Warner, Meadowbrook Press, 1999

Better Homes and Gardens New Baby Book
Carol Keough, Bantam, 1999

Caring for Your Baby and Young Child
American Academy of Pediatrics, Bantam Doubleday, 1998

Dr. Spock's Baby and Child Care
Dr. Benjamin Spock, Pocket Books, 1998

Guide to Baby Products
Sandy Jones, Consumer Reports Books, 2001

First Twelve Months of Life
Frank Caplan, Theresa Caplan, Bantam Books, 1995

First-Year Baby Care
Edited by Dr. Paula Kelly, Meadowbrook Press, 1996

The Girlfriend's Guide to Surviving the First Year of Motherhood
Vicki Iovine, Perigee, 1997

Infants and Mothers: Differences in Development
Dr. T. Berry Brazelton, Delacorte Press, 1994

Parenting: Guide to Your Baby's First Year
Editors of Parenting Magazine, Ballantine, 1999

Sign with Your Baby
Joseph Garcia, Northlight Communications, 2000

Smart Start for Your Baby
Penny Warner, Meadowbrook Press, 2001

Touchpoints: Birth to 3
T. Berry Brazelton, Perseus, 1994

What to Expect the First Year
Arlene Eisenberg, Workman Publishing, 1996

Your Baby's First Year Week by Week
Glade Curtis, M.D., Fisher Books, 2000

Index

Also from Meadowbrook Press

✦ *Play and Learn*
Baby Play and Learn and *Preschooler Play and Learn*, from child-development expert Penny Warner, offer ideas for games and activities that will provide hours of developmental learning opportunities and fun for babies and young children. Each book contains step-by-step instructions, illustrations, and bulleted lists of skills your child will learn through play activities.

✦ *Practical Parenting Tips*
The number one selling collection of helpful hints for parents with babies and small children, containing 1,001 parent-tested tips for dealing with everything from diaper rash, nighttime crying, toilet training, and temper tantrums, to traveling with tots. Parents will save time, trouble, and money.

✦ *Feed Me! I'm Yours*
Parents love this easy-to-use, economical guide to making baby food at home. More than 200 recipes cover everything a parent needs to know about teething foods, nutritious snacks, and quick, pleasing lunches.

✦ *Smart Start for Your Baby*
Child-development expert Penny Warner has written the only baby-care guide that not only helps you understand your baby's physical, cognitive, and psychological growth during each week of his or her first year, but also helps you stimulate your baby's development with hundreds of simple suggestions.

We offer many more titles written to delight, inform, and entertain.

To order books with a credit card or browse our full

selection of titles, visit our web site at:

www.meadowbrookpress.com

or call toll-free to place an order, request a free catalog, or ask a question:

1-800-338-2232

Meadowbrook Press • 5451 Smetana Drive • Minnetonka, MN • 55343